TO

Evelyn

My dear friend

FROM

Kitty

DATE

Christmas 2014

12 STORIES OF CHRISTMAS

by *Robert J. Morgan*

THOMAS NELSON
Since 1798

NASHVILLE   MEXICO CITY   RIO DE JANEIRO

Published in Nashville, Tennessee, by Thomas Nelson.

Published in association with Yates & Yates, www.yates2.com.

Cover and interior design by Koechel Peterson & Associates, Minneapolis, MN

Thomas Nelson titles may be purchased in bulk for educational, business, fund-raising, or sales promotional use. For information, please e-mail SpecialMarkets@ThomasNelson.com.

Unless otherwise noted, Scripture quotations are taken from the KING JAMES VERSION. Scripture quotations marked NIV are taken from THE HOLY BIBLE, NEW INTERNATIONAL VERSION®. Copyright © 1973, 1978, 1984, 2011 by Biblica, Inc.™ Used by permission. All rights reserved worldwide. www.zondervan.com

ISBN-13: 978-0-7180-1196-3

Printed in China

14 15 16 17 RRD 5 4 3 2 1

www.thomasnelson.com

DEDICATED TO LILLIAN RUTH

Table of Contents

Foreword

 have always loved stories. I love to read them, and I love to tell them. I cannot preach without them and—according to my wife—I cannot carry on a conversation without them.

Life is one story made up of many stories . . . the story of our childhood and of our youth . . . the story of our marriage and of the birth of our children . . . the story of our old age and, yes, even the story of our death.

There is something about Christmas that adds to the mystery of stories. I think it has to do with the story of Christmas itself. Could any connected narration of events be as compelling and awe-inspiring as the original, the one found within the pages of the Scriptures?

I believe it is that story that inspires so many other stories at Christmastime. Even those who may not know anything about the story of Christ's birth seem to get caught up in storytelling during the latter days of December.

The late pastor and writer J. B. Phillips wrote:

> *If words are to enter men's minds and bear fruit, they must be the right words shaped cunningly to pass men's defenses and explode silently and effectually within their minds.*

Few people I know have the creativity to shape words like that, but my friend Rob Morgan does. When I read his new collection of Christmas stories, I thought of the blessing they must be to the people who hear them for the first time. Each Christmas Eve, Rob reads a brand-new Christmas story to his congregation at the Donelson Fellowship in Nashville. From what I hear, the congregation considers this one of the highlights of the year.

Rob, it's time you let us in on this Christmas blessing.

—David Jeremiah

That's My Boy!

na Dübendorf leaned against the refrigerator and closed her eyes, oblivious to the commotion around her—pots clanging, cleavers chopping, oil sizzling. Retreating into her own mood, she thought of the twists and turns that had made her a premier chef on the continent, and that had, in their unfolding designs, brought her to this evening—to the final seating of her last night as proprietor of Switzerland's best-known restaurant.

Ana had grown up in Geneva, where her mother was an air traffic controller and her father worked for the United Nations. Neither parent cooked. All their meals were taken at restaurants until Ana, at age eleven, spied a large book in the library, an illustrated cookbook. In opening its pages, she found her future. Soon she was pulling pots and pans from the pantry and making exploratory trips to neighborhood markets. Through trial and error she taught herself to cook.

The next year Ana was cast as the innkeeper's daughter in the Christmas play at Geneva's Central Church. Her job was to bring a jug of soup to Joseph and Mary in the stable after Christ was born. Ana spent days perfecting her Christmas Soup, which she handed to Mary in a pottery mug during the main performance. With the babe in her lap, the Holy Virgin lifted the soup to her mouth, got a whiff of the spices, tasted the luxurious liquid, and drained the cup with a large, unscripted slurp. Forgetting her lines, Mary exclaimed for all to hear: "This is the best soup I've ever tasted!"

At that moment Ana was certain she wanted to be a chef.

After secondary school Ana enrolled in the best cooking institute in Geneva, then went on to culinary school in Paris and Berlin. At twenty-five, her first cookbook, *The Stable Table*, became a best seller, leading to a television program by the same name. When she was thirty, Ana opened The Stable Table, an exclusive restaurant near Langenbruck in the Juro Mountains near the Alps. Although the restaurant was one of Europe's finest, its motif was humble, modeled after the setting of the Christmas play where Ana had discovered her life's calling. The restaurant resembled a rustic stable with wooden beams and half-timbered walls and custom-made lanterns for illumination. It was the epitome of Old World charm, evocative, transporting diners to another world.

As time went by, Ana built a culinary empire. She never married; she loved her work more than anything. But time took a toll. At fifty-five she suffered a mild heart attack—too much butter and cream, said doctors; too much stress and strain, said friends—and the ensuing depression left her ready to retire and spend her days working quietly on revisions to her cookbooks with publisher Klaus Adler of Munich. After tonight's eight o'clock seating, The Stable Table would lock its doors as Ana Dübendorf retreated from public view.

❄ ❄ ❄

Marco broke her contemplation. "Ana," he said, "the first sleigh is entering the gate. Time to meet the guests."

Ana made her way to the porch as the first horse-drawn sleigh arrived with the occupants of Table Number One—Bruno Bergin, famed Vienna opera star, and his wife, Therese. The rotund, pompous Bruno swung theatrically from the carriage with cape and cane, his thick black hair tossed by the wind. "Bruno!" said Ana. "Therese! Come in. Marco will take your coats and give you some hot soup from the sideboard."

The Bergins ambled into the restaurant with a nod and a scowl. Watching them, Ana wondered how Therese could live with a man famous for his foul moods. But of course, there was the fame and the acclaim; there was the money.

As Marco seated the Bergins by the window, Ana prepared to greet the next guests—Private First Class Hubert Holloway of the United States Army, stationed at Wiesbaden, and his wealthy Aunt Louise Berkley from Chicago's North Shore. Hubert was his aunt's sole heir, but the relationship was strained. The original quarrel had involved Hubert's father, but the grievance had spanned a generation. Now the elegant, elderly woman was in Europe for the holidays, hoping to repair the breach. They were seated at Table Two near the sideboard.

The third sleigh bore a single occupant, Ana's publisher, the recently widowed Klaus Adler. The distinguished gentleman from Munich with gray hair and trim mustache emerged from the carriage with a warm greeting: "How are you, dear?"

"I don't know, Klaus," Ana said honestly. "I'm just concentrating on tonight. How are you?"

"It's been lonely," he replied. "But we can chat later. I'm staying in the village a few days. But Ana, quickly, I want to tell you. An idea came to me while riding up the hill—almost an epiphany as I saw The Stable Table lit up through the snow."

"Yes?" Ana said.

"You must not close this restaurant," said Klaus. "Let's keep it

open—but maybe just one day a year. Think of it! You can have seatings all day on Christmas, breakfast to midnight. It'll give you something to plan each year. We can build a cookbook around the idea, maybe a television special. I'll help you."

"Oh my," said Ana, "I've never thought of such a thing, and I can't think of it now. Look, here comes Table Four. Help me greet them, Klaus."

The next sleigh glided to a halt, and out lumbered the evening's most unlikely guests—a medical school dropout named Brigitte Gallio, who lived in Dijon, and her brother Philippe, a photographer from Genoa whose camera hung from his shoulder like a permanent attachment. The brother and sister, both unemployed, had won their reservations in a contest. They were clad in threadbare coats and rough hats, but Ana put them at ease and Klaus accompanied them into the restaurant, chatting to them as if to old friends.

Table Five arrived next—Arthur and Isabelle Blanc, a young jet-setting couple with royal blood in their veins. Ana frequently saw their pictures in magazines. Jumping athletically from the sleigh, Arthur assisted his glamorous wife, who was quite pregnant. From newspaper reports Ana knew the child—their first, a boy—was due in early February.

The occupants of Table Six were Ana's friends, Johannes and Emmalina Mossman, circus owners from Berne. Their show horses were the ones drawing the sleds up the hill. Ana had rented them for the night. These were the finest steeds in Europe, especially a four-year-old Andalusian named That's My Boy, the horse of a thousand tricks. He was a favorite at fairs and festivals across Europe, but tonight he was on sleigh duty alongside his fellow horses, making guests feel they were being swept into a Currier and Ives painting. Yet Ana knew the Swiss Traveling Circus was in trouble. Bookings had fallen off; expenses were high. Even amid the cheer of the holiday, she saw the strain on the face of her friend Johannes.

Table Seven belonged to Sébastien Brahms from Zurich, a former banker who battled depression. His family was gone, his friends were few, his health was failing, and his money was running low. Those who knew him called him Sad Sébastien, for he had forgotten how to laugh.

And so they came, more and more, table by table, arriving in a parade of jingling sleighs drawn by circus horses, gliding over the mountain pass and through the deepening snow. It was a fairy-tale night in the foothills of the Alps of Switzerland.

After the final guests were seated and drinks poured, a small

army of white-clad servers entered the room, bearing aloft platters that descended to each table like flying saucers making orchestrated landings. The room hummed with "ahs" and "ohs" as food was ladled onto dishes, and the din of conversation gave way to the clinking of silver to china. The spirit of Christmas settled into the room like the very fragrance of joy.

But that's when everything went wrong.

The problem started at Table Two, when Private First Class Hubert Holloway was halfway through the opening course. "This is delicious," he said, dabbing his mouth and smiling for the first time. "I wonder what it is?"

"It's called boris-crowder," his aunt said nonchalantly. "I've had it occasionally, but never as good as this."

"I've never heard of boris-crowder," said the soldier. "What's in it?"

"It's a mixture of meat wrapped in casings and fried till it's crispy."

"But what kind of meat?" asked the soldier. "I've never tasted anything like it."

"Well, if you must know," said Aunt Louise, "it's rabbit. It's small bits of rabbit organs—bunny brains and tongues and hearts—encased in their intestines and fried in their own fat."

The simple words of that sentence hit Private First Class Holloway

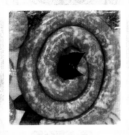

like bombshells exploding in slow motion. His face went white, then took on a green hue. His eyes lost focus. The regions of his stomach felt rising turbulence. A reaction seized him as violent and as sudden as a volcano, and as unstoppable. Nothing like this had happened to him before. He was taken by surprise.

So was Aunt Louise. Seeing disaster hurtling toward her, the woman leaped from the table like a pedestrian vaulting from the path of a runaway car. Losing balance as her oaken chair flew backward, she landed on the sideboard, striking the soup tureen with the force of a baseball bat. With a mighty crash, the whole table collapsed—soups and drinks and ice and china tumbling downward like an avalanche. The noise was deafening.

Conversation in the room ceased as if frozen in midair. Ana Dübendorf and her staff—every cook, server, apprentice, busboy, and dishwasher—rushed to the calamity with feelings of horror. The humiliated soldier and his aunt made mortified exits to the bathrooms while the kitchen crew ran for mops and towels and buckets.

No sooner had employees cleared away the mess than another

misfortune arose. Smoke billowed from the kitchen, triggering smoke alarms like emergency sirens. "Something's burning!" Marco shouted. The whole staff—every cook, server, apprentice, busboy, and dishwasher—raced back to the kitchen to face the fire. It was caused by untended rabbit grease splattering onto the burners. Out came the fire extinguishers, and with great plumes of vapor, the flames were doused. The alarms fell silent, and Ana Dübendorf, disheveled and shaken, reentered the dining room with an announcement.

"Friends," she said coughing, "we had a little fire on the stove, but it's extinguished and we're safe. So is the food. There will be a slight delay before the next course; please bear with us. We'll open the windows to clear the air. In the interval, if you need your coat, Marco will fetch it. I apologize for the inconvenience. Dinner will resume presently."

Like an army regrouping from a defeat, busboys mobilized toward the large windows, throwing them wide open, including the one behind the famous opera star Bruno Bergin, who in turn barked an order to Marco: "Young man, bring my cape and cane!"

"Yes sir, at once!" said Marco, heading toward the checkroom. But he had taken only a few steps when another catastrophe occurred. Johannes, the circus owner, glancing in the direction of Bruno Bergin's barking order, jumped to his feet, eyes wide with dismay. Pointing to the window, he shouted, "That's My Boy!"

But it was too late. That's My Boy, the horse of a thousand tricks, smelling the food and spying an audience, had stuck his head through

the large window. His long, grinning yellow teeth descended right onto Bruno Bergin's scalp. In one seamless swoop the horse pulled a thick mane of black hair from the top of the great tenor's head. Bruno, it turned out, was bald as a boulder.

"That's My Boy!" Johannes again shouted in alarm.

At that moment a flash blinded the diners. It was from the camera of the unemployed photographer Philippe Gallio. Bruno lunged beneath the table and hid like a child under the tablecloth while Philippe, now on his feet and running around the room, kept snapping, his flash cutting the room like strobe lights.

Johannes Mossman was on his feet too, tearing after his horse like a tornado, jumping out the open window and running through the snow, shouting, "That's My Boy! That's My Boy!"

Watching all this unfold like a distorted fantasy, Sad Sébastien at Table Seven felt an unexpected chuckle. He stopped himself, but it came again like a hiccup. He began giggling like a girl, then laughing like a drunken fool. He laughed till it hurt and his eyes filled with tears; still, he couldn't control himself. His mirth was infectious. It spread from table to table, and soon everyone was holding their sides and wiping their eyes with Ana's white linen napkins.

But the worst was yet to come. Endeavoring to evade the laughter, Bruno wrapped his head in the tablecloth like a Middle Eastern sheik and made a dash for it, dragging place settings and china behind him with sickening crashes. Boris-crowder rolled across the floor like marbles. *Pop* went another flash; and Bruno, in a state of disorientation, tripped over his tablecloth and tumbled into Table Five, which was occupied by Arthur and Isabelle Blanc, the young jet-setting couple awaiting the birth of their first child.

They didn't have to wait long. Isabelle, who had been laughing convulsively, now rolled onto the floor trying to dodge the descending Bruno. Hitting the hardwood, she felt sudden surges of constrictions and contractions that told her the time had come.

"Arthur," she cried, "the baby! I think he's coming."

"Is there a doctor in the house?" hollered Arthur.

"That's My Boy!" came a shout through the open window.

"I'm a nurse," said Brigitte, medical-school dropout from Dijon. "Well, not technically, but I've had training. I can help. Someone call an ambulance!"

"The snow is too deep for an ambulance," said a voice.

"We'll have to take her down by sled," said another.

But it was too late for that. Isabelle was helped to a side room, and there, aided by Brigitte, little Arthur William Harry Blanc made his debut at 9:47 p.m. on Christmas Day. When the sound of the baby's cry wafted into the dining room, the tension eased, a cheer went up, and there was a soft and grateful round of applause. The Munich publisher Klaus Adler spoke for all when he said, "Thanks be to God!"

It took a long time for medical personnel to reach The Stable Table. In the interval, That's My Boy was corralled, the horses were re-harnessed, and the guests were delivered down the hill. Meanwhile Ana Dübendorf brought a hot cup of Christmas Soup to the new mother. In trembling hands and with the baby in her lap, Isabelle Blanc lifted the mug to her mouth, got a whiff of the spices, tasted the luxurious liquid, and drained the cup with a slurp. "This is the best soup I've ever tasted!" she said.

Ana beamed as if life had been reborn.

It took time for the patrons of The Stable Table to recover from the events of that never-to-be forgotten night. But in looking back, they all agreed: everything that evening worked for the best of all concerned.

Philippe sold his pictures to the leading tabloids of Europe, putting his career as a photojournalist on the fast track. The photographs and accompanying stories became the buzz of the media for a full week, during the slow-news days between Christmas and New Year's.

❧

Philippe's sister, medical-school dropout Brigitte Gallio of Dijon, decided to give nursing another try, encouraged by the success of her Christmas Day delivery.

Bruno Bergin benefited from his lesson in humility. For a change, he listened to his wife when she told him not to take himself too seriously. Besides, his picture appeared in the world's leading tabloids; and for an opera singer, any publicity is good publicity.

Private First Class Hubert Holloway was nursed through Christmas night by Aunt Louise, and by the next day they laughed every time they recalled their story. Whatever disagreement had threatened them, it was never again mentioned. The two bonded like buddies in a foxhole.

Circus owners Johannes and Emmalina Mossman, aided by the notoriety, encountered no further problems with bookings. That's My Boy performed to capacity crowds who laughed uproariously when the horse came onstage in a large wig and pretended to sing while a majestic operatic voice boomed through the speakers.

Sad Sébastien returned to Zurich with a dose of the best medicine in the world—the elixir of laughter.

Little Arthur William Harry Blanc gained weight rapidly and seemed to thrive despite his precarious beginning.

And as for The Stable Table, well, it *had* to remain open—at least for one more Christmas, because all the guests received rainchecks.

❄ ❄ ❄

And so it was—to Ana's delight—that every single patron reassembled exactly one year later, all at their original tables, for the eight o'clock seating. Everyone showed up as if no time had passed at all. Everything was exactly the same, with the exception of boris-crowder—which was forever stricken from the menu—and the dessert, which this year was a large Black Forest cake in honor of the youngest guest who was celebrating his first birthday.

Taking little Arthur William Harry in her arms at the end of the meal, Ana led the guests in a round of "Happy Birthday" and hugged the child with great affection. When he giggled at her, she giggled back and said proudly, "That's my boy!"

To which Klaus Adler replied, "Thanks be to God."

And on that magical night in the snow-draped Juro mountains of Switzerland, at the eight o'clock seating of The Stable Table, everyone

pondered the great mystery they had all experienced in the intervening year, and the lesson they had learned: no matter what goes wrong in life or what disasters befall us, the birth of a little boy in a rustic stable on Christmas Day somehow makes everything turn out just right.

Ollie

I am going to tell you a story, just as my father told it to me, for I can still remember almost word for word how he related it to me on Christmas Eve of 1963. We had finished dinner, opened some presents, and put on our pajamas. Just before bedtime, as the last log was burning in the fireplace, I saw my dad walk over to the mantel. He took down the antique snow globe with its small nativity scene and turned the crank on the bottom. The little music box played "Silent Night" as the snow swirled around Joseph, Mary, and the baby in the manger. My dad was lost in thought until the music ceased, then he turned and saw me watching him. I guess I looked at him quizzically, because he went on to recite a little poem I'd never heard before, as though he were explaining something to me.

Silent, holy, calm, and bright,

Jesus came to pierce the night.

Jesus came to make things right.

So be . . .

Silent, holy, calm, and bright,

. . . tonight.

I didn't know what to make of it, so I did what most twelve-year-olds would do. I asked questions. "What d'ya mean, Dad? Where'd you get that old globe anyhow? Where'd it come from?"

Well, he sat right down on the floor, there in front of the fireplace with the snow globe resting in his lap, and he motioned for me. I sat down beside him, and he turned the thing over and showed me what was stamped on the bottom: *Made in Germany, 1938.* Then he put his arm around me, and this is what he said:

❋ ❋ ❋

Something interesting happened to me, son, when I was your age, when I was twelve years old. It was in 1942. We were living in a little town called Evergreen, Pennsylvania, where my dad had a law practice. Well, that year was unusually busy, and my folks waited until the last possible day—December 24—to do gift buying. It was about midmorning when we drove downtown, plunged into the crowds on Main Street, and did all

our shopping in one giant trip. Of course, there wasn't much shopping to do back then. World War II was going on, and things were hard to come by. That year we just bought a few items for each other. My dad found a simple necklace for Mom; she bought him a tie and a pair of socks; and, from the size of the package, I suspicioned that my gift was a new pair of shoes. We also found a red sweater for my grandma.

We loaded those gifts into the trunk of our 1938 Buick, which we'd left in the town parking lot. Then we walked back to the corner market where we managed to find everything we needed for Christmas dinner—a canned ham (the only kind available in those days), some cloves and spices, baking potatoes, beans, and carrots. And then some flour, butter, eggs, sugar, and chocolate for a cake. I remember how relieved my mother was to find some of those staples—they were rationed because of the war, you see. After loading everything in the car, we walked down the street one more time and ate a late lunch at the Evergreen Café.

You can imagine our surprise when we returned to the parking lot an hour later and could not find our car. It was gone, vanished, along with our presents and all our food. Someone had stolen our vehicle—

and with it they had taken our Christmas. We spent the afternoon in the police station filling out reports, talking to the officers, and listening while they issued bulletins. But it was useless. No one had a clue what had happened to our Buick. My folks were very distressed. The officers said they'd drive us home, but we said we'd just as soon walk, as we only lived a few blocks away. By then it was late on the afternoon of Christmas Eve, and the snow was flurrying. So down the street we started, wondering how we were going to celebrate Christmas with no presents and no dinner. Most of the stores had closed, and the shoppers had gone home. We passed the parking lot, and it was empty—almost.

There to our amazement sat our car.

It was on the opposite side of the parking lot. My parents looked at each other in confusion, and we all said things like, "Are we losing our minds?" "Did we forget where we parked?" "I'm sure we parked over here." "Who moved our car over there?"

We walked over to investigate. At first glance it appeared that whoever had moved our car had also washed and cleaned it, for it looked newer and neater than before. But the thief had also cleaned out all our gifts because when my dad opened the trunk, it was empty. We unlocked the doors, got in, and sat there like we were in a fog.

Finally my mom said, "Thomas, this is not our car."

"No," said my dad, "it isn't, is it? But it looks like it." He turned the key in the ignition, and the engine started.

Well, in those days the Detroit carmakers had a limited number of keys and locks, and they were often interchangeable. I remember once my mother locked her keys in the car at school. Another teacher said, "I own a Buick too. Let's see if my key fits your car." And it did. So that explained why the key worked, but it explained nothing else.

My mom opened the glove compartment and found the registration. She said, "This car belongs to Alfreda Reinhart, 508 Elm Street."

"I know her," said my dad. "Well, at least I met her once. I think she's a bit daft. You know, not all there. Do you suppose she could have driven off in our car by mistake?"

"Well, I don't know," said Mom. "I heard some ladies talking about her. It's a sad story. Alfreda is quite elderly. When she lived in Germany, her family was thrown into jail for opposing the National Socialists. She had a son, a daughter-in-law, and a little grandson, a boy of about twelve or so. Some kind of disease swept through the jail, and the whole family died, except Alfreda. After she was released, she managed to leave Germany. Then she moved here to Evergreen where her sister lived, over near the German Lutheran Church. When her sister died,

Alfreda seemed to go senile. At least, that's what they said in the beauty shop."

"Yes, and as I recall, she's as deaf as a doornail," said my dad. "And I guess that would explain things. Our cars look alike, the keys are interchangeable, and she must have gotten in the wrong one by mistake. Let's go see."

Well, this was turning into an exciting Christmas for me—a stolen car, an imprisoned family, a crazy old woman, and all our Christmas presents hanging in the balance. It was an adventure!

So off we drove; and ten minutes later we pulled into the driveway at 508 Elm Street. There was our car, all right, sitting in Mrs. Reinhart's carport. We got out and peered in the car windows and opened the trunk. It was empty.

We rang the doorbell, and presently a little hunched lady opened the door. Her hair was thin, white, and disheveled, which was also a description of her. An old pair of glasses sat crookedly on her nose. She wore a faded blue sweater. On seeing us, she burst into joyous smiles. "*Guten Abend!*," she cried. "*Guten Abend!* Come in out of the cold! Come in out of the snow! Right on time you are, right on time!"

We stepped into the house. It was rather dark and drafty, but a small fire was burning in the hearth and a little tree sat in the corner. Underneath it were some presents that looked very much like the ones we had bought earlier in the day. I also got a whiff of supper. It smelled

like ham with cloves, along with potatoes, carrots, beans, and cake. On the mantle was a snow globe nestled among some garland. I took it all in with a glance.

"Now, give me your coat, Gunther, and you too, Elke," said the old woman. "Oh, how vonderful to see you."

"Frau Reinhart," said my dad, clearing his throat, "I've come to tell you we've mixed up our cars."

Mrs. Reinhart seemed to have trouble understanding, so my dad repeated himself. "We've mixed up our cars."

She looked perplexed. "*Vas?*" she said.

"Our cars!" said Dad.

"Cigars? *Ja*, I have cigars. Would you like one?"

"No, no," said my father quickly.

"You always liked your cigars, Gunther," the woman said, shaking her head with a smile. "I try to keep them for you. But for after supper, not before, *ja*?"

"No, no," said Dad. "What I mean is, I think there's been some kind of mistake."

"*Ja*, of course I have cake too," she said.

"No, no, Frau Reinhart," said my dad, trying a third time, "I'm afraid you're confused. My name is Vicker. Thomas Vicker."

Something about that seemed to distress the old woman. Alfreda Reinhart stared at my dad incredulously, a haunting look on her face, as if trying to comprehend. For some reason, we all sort of stopped breathing for a moment.

"*Nein*," she said.

Again my father said, "Frau Reinhart, my name is Thomas Vicker. Vicker."

"*Nein*, I have no liquor," she said. "I have cigars and cake, but no liquor. Only eggnog." My dad was too flabbergasted to reply, but the atmosphere changed suddenly when the old woman smiled, showing yellow unkempt teeth. "*Sehr gut*," she said, "Your coats. *Bitten*. It's warm in here. Let me help your coats. I've vaited so long for you to get here. I've vaited all afternoon. You're going to stay, aren't you? Of course you are. You've come so far."

She started tugging at sleeves, and I noticed how my parents looked at each other and seemed to reach a kind of understanding. At any rate, they nodded to me, and we all unbuttoned our coats.

"*Danke*," said the old woman, with a smile. She took Dad's coat and Mom's and laid them on the sofa, and that's when she spied me.

I cannot describe the look that came into her eyes as she studied my face. "Oh, Ollie," she said, hobbling near me. Her hand revealed a slight tremor as it reached out and caressed my hair. "Oh, my Ollie, it has been so long. Look at you! Look how you've grown."

Her eyes filled with tears as she pulled me into an embrace. She quivered with emotion, but when she released me, her face was glowing. "Oh, Ollie," she said, "I thought I vould never see you again. Come over to your *oma*. And look at you, so happy and so strong and so big! You so remind me of your *opa*."

Her wiry arms encircled me again, and I felt her kissing the top of my head. I started to pull away, but I didn't. After one more, "My Ollie," she turned abruptly and headed to the kitchen.

"*Aber was den!* All is ready," she said. "Elke, help me set the table." My mom obligingly found some dishes in the cabinet, while Frau Reinhart pulled silverware from a drawer. Then out came the ham and the beans and carrots, along with a German potato salad and some sauerkraut. The meal wasn't as my mom would have prepared it. It was sort of vinegary and mustardy, but it was good, and I ate every bite—except the kraut.

All the while, Frau Reinhart was talking, half in German, half in English, about family matters that didn't make any sense at all to me. Each of us tried to contribute to the conversation, but it seemed lost on the old woman. Her hearing was gone, and her mind nearly so. But her heart was warm, and she kept the conversation flowing all by herself. She spoke of long ago days, recalling happier times with Dietrich—her husband, I gathered—and with her son, Gunther, who had apparently been a bookkeeper, and his wife, Elke. Occasionally she said something that seemed funny to her, and she laughed and laughed, and we laughed along with her.

All the while she kept stealing glances in my direction, and whenever she did her eyes sparkled. A couple of times I winked at her, and she seemed as delighted as a girl caught under the mistletoe.

After the cake and coffee—the eggnog never showed up—we relocated to the parlor where Mrs. Reinhart went right to the tree and started handing out gifts. There was a simple necklace for my mom, a tie and socks for my dad, and a pair of new shoes for me. It was all great fun. Then my mother handed the last remaining package to the old woman. Frau Reinhart opened the present and clutched the red sweater to herself with motions of delight.

"Oh, *danke, danke*! It is *wunderbar*," she said. "But the most vonderful thing is to have you all here with me." Then she lowered her voice almost to a whisper and said, "One night, in that awful place, I was so frightened, especially for Ollie. I had forgotten what time of year it vas, all vas so dark and so dreadful. Everyone vas so sick. And then from somewhere down the hall, I heard another prisoner singing, 'Silent night, holy night, all is calm, all is bright . . .' And I recalled that it was Christmas. And that night in the jail, I remembered a little poem we used to say on Christmas Eve:

> *Silent, holy, calm, and bright,*
> *Jesus came to pierce the night.*
> *Jesus came to make things right.*
> *So be . . .*
> *Silent, holy, calm, and bright,*
> *. . . tonight.*

"And that's when I knew that everything vould be all right, someday, somehow, someway, someplace. Perhaps not now, but then; perhaps not here, but there."

She was quiet for a moment. But the next thing I knew, she was on her feet again and headed to the fireplace. She picked up the snow globe from the mantle and shook it in our direction, saying, "Except for the clothes on my back, this is the only I thing I brought with me out of *Deutschland*."

She wound up the music, and it played "Silent Night." We listened and it seemed like music from far away and long ago. No one said anything for a long time. Then the old woman, suddenly looking very tired, said, "Vell, it is time for bed. Oh, it vould have broken my heart had you not come. But here you are! And my Ollie has come to wish his *oma* a *Frohe Weihnachten*. God bless you for it, my grandson."

I nodded as best I could. We rose, put on our coats, and moved toward the door.

"Vait!" called the old woman. She picked up the globe and brought it to me. "You must have this, Ollie," she said. "It's the only thing I can give you from *Deutschland*, and you must take it so you'll always remember that God looked into our globe and saw our grief. We look in His manger and see His answer."

Well, I looked at Dad, he looked at Mom, and she looked at me. I took the globe from the woman's hands, sat it on the floor, and gave her

the hardest hug I'd given anyone in my life. Then I picked it up carefully and ducked out the door because no one wants to see a twelve-year-old boy get the sniffles.

I heard my parents exiting behind me, saying things like, "*Gute Nacht*" and "*Auf Wiedersehen,*" and after exchanging cars in the carport, we drove home in silence.

We visited Frau Reinhart several times afterward, but she didn't seem to know us. The spell was broken, and her mind was gone. Shortly afterward, a small item appeared in the local paper:

> *Frau Alfreda Reinhart, 88, formerly of Munich, died at her residence on Elm Street yesterday with her parish priest in attendance. She was preceded in death by a husband, a sister, a son, a daughter-in-law, and a grandson.*

❄ ❄ ❄

Well, that's the story as my dad told it to me. But he wasn't quite finished. He went on to say, "And that's why, son, every year since I was your age, I've picked up this old globe on Christmas Eve, turned it over, wound it up, and listened to its music. And as I see the snow swirling around the manger, I think of the night my folks and I were able to give an old woman her family back for one last Christmas Eve. And I remember her poem and her words, for they are true. The good Lord looked into our globe and saw our grief. We look into His manger and see His answer. And that's why Christmas is silent and holy and calm and bright."

For a long time we sat there in front of the dying fire, saying nothing. I might have gotten the sniffles if my dad hadn't told me that no one wanted to see a twelve-year-old boy do that. So I finally got up, yawned real big, and headed to bed. After all, I didn't want to oversleep on Christmas morning.

"Good night, Dad," I said as I headed toward the bedroom. I turned back and saw him gazing again at that glass ball filled with water and wonder. "Good night, Dad," I said again. "Sleep well."

He smiled and waved me on to bed. "Good night, Ollie," he said. "You sleep well too."

Mainely Christmas

alph Hannaford stood at the railing of his darkened porch, binoculars in hand, like a ship's captain gazing into the night. He muttered to himself as he studied the revelers across the intersection. The Winter Solstice Festival in Freeport, Maine, had spilled beyond the park and into the streets. Everyone came from near and far, turning the town square into a wonderland. Children frolicked in colorful overcoats. A jazz band played carols on the corner. Saint Nicholas posed for pictures beneath the Sailors and Soldiers Monument. Bonfires blazed. Lights twinkled from trees. Open-air vendors hawked lobster rolls and steaming cups of New England clam chowder.

Ralph inspected the mayhem from the porch of the house where he'd been born sixty-two years before—a captain's house, faded green, Victorian, built by his paternal grandfather, who was a shipbuilder.

Ralph's father had been a lobsterman, but Ralph wanted nothing to do with the sea and never went down to the harbor. For most of his life he'd worked at L.L. Bean, the famous outfitter and Freeport's primary employer. He had mixed feelings about it. He enjoyed being close enough to walk to work, but he hated how retailers had overtaken Freeport with outlet stores and tourist traps. A toyshop now occupied the city's historic library. The town hall had become meeting space for a hotel. The old café with its twenty-five-cent cups of java had become a trendy coffee shop with five-dollar shots of espresso. Even the lobster boats in the harbor, currently bedecked with strings of holiday lights, were mostly for tourists wanting to see the lighthouses Down East.

"Ayuh," Ralph muttered, "if I didn't have two acres behind this old house, and my dog, Roxie and my little flock of sheep, I'd lose my mind. Especially this time of year." Standing at the end of his porch, Ralph again raised his binoculars to inspect his sheep, wondering how it was that he—a man who didn't believe in Christmas—had lent them to the nativity scene on the far corner of the square.

❄ ❄ ❄

On the far corner of the square, the town's young cardiologist, Dr. Sam Scott, was dressed like biblical Joseph. He greeted passersby with a gentle smile and a fake beard. His wife, Edie, stood nearby, playing the role of Mary. Their four-month-old Walter was wrapped up as baby Jesus. The Christ child should have been in the manger, but it was hard to get him out of the arms of Edie's overbearing mother, the plump and outspoken Gloria Eagleburger, who was decked out as an angel.

A small menagerie of barnyard animals encircled the holy family—two calves, five sheep, a herding dog named Roxie, a donkey, and a grumpy llama named Mildred.

"I don't know why we have a llama," Gloria complained. "Whoever heard of a llama in a nativity scene?"

"Don't gripe about it," Dr. Scott said. "He came with the donkey. Plus, it's the closest I could find to a camel."

"A llama is nothing like a camel."

"They're a little alike," said the doctor.

"*Humph!*" Gloria said. "The only thing they have in common is that they both spit at you."

Cutting her a glance, Dr. Scott said, "This is no time to get your halo bent, Gloria. Let's just be thankful we're able to do this at all. It took a lot of effort to pull off this nativity display."

It *had* taken a determined spirit to gain approval for the living crèche in Freeport's town square. With Gloria's aid, Dr. Scott had mounted a campaign for including it in the annual Solstice Festival. Sam and Gloria didn't always get along—she referred to him as "my son-in-law the cardiologist"—but the nativity campaign had made them allies, with Gloria spearheading a petition drive while Dr. Scott lobbied the town council. They were so successful that the city fathers had asked for two presentations—one during the Solstice Festival and

another two nights later on Christmas Eve to add to the atmosphere of Freeport's final holiday shopping spree.

The breakthrough had come when Ralph Hannaford had dropped his objections to the endeavor. He even offered to loan his five sheep to the cause. He wasn't thrilled about it, but everyone knew Ralph owed his life to Dr. Scott, who had been standing behind him at the coffee shop five years before when Ralph collapsed with chest pains after paying for his espresso.

And so on December 22, at the far corner of Freeport's Town Square, a rustic shed housed the holy family and an odd assortment of livestock, including a small flock of sheep.

※ ※ ※

From the secluded corner of his front porch, Ralph watched headlights moving down the street like strings of luminescent marbles. Through his binoculars he checked once more on his flock. Ralph was more curious than worried. He had sent Roxie with them, and there wasn't a better sheep dog in New England. Roxie would keep a close eye on the flock and herd them back at evening's end. Then she'd close the gate with her nose and curl up in the doorway of the barn where she always spent the night. Still, Ralph couldn't rest until he knew his sheep were safely in the fold.

His attention was suddenly drawn to the sound of his gate snapping open and shut. Footsteps pattered up the sidewalk. Ralph turned, binoculars still to his eyes, and the lens filled with the form of a large, middle-aged angel who smiled at him.

"Ralph, I know you're there. I spied you a half hour ago. Open the front door for me. I have to change baby Jesus."

"Look at this crowd," Ralph said petulantly as he put down the binoculars and opened the door for Gloria Eagleburger and the baby. "And look at you," he said, studying her white gown with wings attached at the shoulders and a halo around her head. "What's that stain on your robe here? Did the baby poop on you?"

"Of course not. Mildred spat on me."

"Who's Mildred?"

"The llama."

"Sounds like loads of fun," Ralph chuckled as he watched Gloria unwrap the baby on the end of the sofa.

"Well, Ralph, it *is* fun," said Gloria. "You should go over and get into the spirit of things. You'd have a wonderful time if you'd let yourself."

"I wouldn't mind having a cup of chowder," he said, "but I'm not going to fight those mobs to get it. You know I don't believe in Christmas."

"Ralph, the past is past," Gloria said as she stripped Walter down to his diaper. "I know very well what happened to you on Christmas Eve, and I grieve for you. I really do. But that was a long time ago—fifty years ago, for goodness sake. At some point we have to move on."

Ralph said nothing, so Gloria kept talking. "I buried my husband on Thanksgiving Day, but I still celebrate Thanksgiving, don't I? We have to go on living, Ralph. We ought to enjoy life as long as God keeps us here."

"You keep talking like that and you'll make me wicked mad."

"Oh, Ralph. Christmas is a season of good tidings and great joy. I'm sorry about what happened to you, but you've taken it out on Christmas long enough. Get over it. Do you have any wipes?"

"Wipes?"

"Baby wipes?"

"Why would I have baby wipes around here?"

"Well, get me a warm washcloth. I wish you'd turn on your porch light. I nearly tripped coming up your steps in the dark, and I was carrying baby Jesus."

Ralph disappeared into the bathroom and returned with a washcloth. "Why should I turn on the lights?" he asked. "Do you think I want thousands of people gawking over here? I wish they'd all go home. I don't believe in any of it."

"*Humph!*" exclaimed Gloria, struggling to get Walter's chubby arms back into his swaddling clothes.

"Let me ask you something," said Ralph. "If there really is a Christmas Spirit, why did *The Lobsterman's Friend* go down on Christmas Eve? On Christmas Eve, of all times! In the Nor'easter! The whole crew! I've never understood that and I never will."

Gloria rolled up the dirty diaper and pointed it at Ralph like a gun. "I don't know, Ralph," she said. "Nobody understands. But I know one thing. I believe in Christmas because that's the only thing that gives us hope when our loved ones die, and when our children run away, and when ships are lost at sea. Now if you want to stand on the porch in the dark and spy on people celebrating Christmas, that's your business. But

as for me, well, I've got to get baby Jesus back to the manger before my son-in-law the cardiologist comes looking for us."

She bundled the baby and headed to the door.

"I wasn't spying!" Ralph called after her. "I was just checking on my sheep! You would have known that if you were a real angel."

"*Humph!*" Gloria exclaimed, disappearing through the door and down the steps.

Her departure had a strange effect on Ralph. The room felt empty after she left. The strains of "O Holy Night" filtered through the walls and sounded like music from another world. A car honked. A child shouted. A horse whinnied. Walking to the mantel, Ralph picked up a small, framed picture of a grinning boy standing beside his dad at the harbor. In the background was an old boat bearing the words *The Lobsterman's Friend*. The man's hair was gray and grizzled under a black cap and his face was weathered, but his arm rested across the boy's shoulders.

"I don't believe in Christmas," Ralph mumbled to himself, replacing the picture.

For the next hour he puttered around the house, worked on a crossword puzzle, threw out some old magazines, poured himself a glass of milk, and killed time till the crowds went home and the noise faded outside his window. Presently he donned his coat and returned to the lookout point on his front porch. He thought of what Gloria had said. *Imagine her telling me to get over it!*

As he turned to reenter the house, he caught a reflection of himself in the windowpanes. He saw an old man with gray and grizzled hair under a black cap. His jacket was faded and frayed. But the rest of the window sparkled with the reflections of the lights and bonfires across the street. Only his own image was dark and brooding.

Impulsively, immediately, inexplicably, Ralph knew it was time at last to face the grief that had haunted him for fifty years. He knew he had to act at once, before he changed his mind. Like a man jumping into a cold lake, Ralph stiffened his resolve and strode to the kitchen, through the storage room, and into the attached barn. He moved quickly, not daring to stop. It was now or never.

He heaved the old wooden ladder from one side of the loft to the other and sat his foot purposefully on the first rung. Climbing to the loft, he shoved aside bales of hay until he uncovered a box that had sat undisturbed for half a century. It was his father's footlocker, a small chest of memories and mustiness. He recalled watching his mother pack it on a snowy New Year's Day long ago, and he still remembered its contents. Pictures. Albums. Ship's logs. Clippings. Bits of debris recovered from *The Lobsterman's Friend*.

Posturing himself in a kneeling position, Ralph gripped the trunk by its leather handle and gave a tug. It didn't move at first, but a second tug yielded results. The chest slid toward him an inch. Ralph shuffled back and tugged again. Inch by inch, foot by foot, he backed toward the ladder, pulling the chest after him. Presently his foot felt the edge of the loft, and Ralph reached backward for the ladder.

Swinging his legs around, he planted his feet on one of the rungs and gripped the top one. He gave the chest another tug. It was heavier than he recalled, and for a moment he wondered if he could maneuver it down the ladder. But he took no time to think. Any pause, any hesitation, and he knew he would give up the endeavor and never try again.

He gave the locker a sharp yank, and as its weight tilted against him, he lost his footing. His hands released their grip. Ralph tumbled backward, the ladder sliding to the right while he toppled to the left. He screamed. It was a high-pitched yell that echoed in the little barn as Ralph plunged nine feet to the dirt floor, striking his head on the side of a stall just as the trunk struck him in the ribs. As Ralph drifted into unconsciousness, he somehow dreamed he was on *The Lobsterman's Friend*, sinking in the cold Christmas Eve waters of Casco Bay.

Across the street, the funnel cake maker poured the last of his batter into his oil, people drifted toward their cars, musicians started packing

up their instruments, and Roxie jumped to her feet. She pricked up her ears, cocked her head, and stared in the direction of home.

* * *

The odor of manure and hay filled the nostrils of the man who didn't believe in Christmas. He opened his eyes, the effort producing a wave of nausea, to see he was in a stable, dimly lit. Everything was blurry and shadowy. His eyes focused just enough to see a small book lying beside him near the manger. It was a little Mariner's New Testament. A flash of recognition trigged a dormant memory in Ralph's benumbed brain, and his eyes lingered on the page that had fallen open: "For unto you is born this day . . ." He scanned the stable around him, hurting and haunted, as his eyelids grew heavy and closed.

He was roused back to consciousness by the sound of a dog barking. *Ruff . . . ruff . . . ralf . . . ralph . . . Ralph!*

Opening his eyes again, he saw the face of Joseph of the Bible there in the dim stable, kneeling over him, calling his name, eyes full of concern. A robe enfolded Joseph's body like corrugated marble, and a cowl encircled his face so completely that Ralph could only really make out his eyes, which were alert and compassionate.

Beside Joseph stood the Virgin Mary. There was no doubt about it. She looked like a Christmas card, radiant, yet with lines of anxiety etched on her face. Why was that? And who was standing nearby? An angel!—the most matronly angel Ralph had ever seen, beautiful for her age. Ralph involuntarily turned his gaze in the direction of the feeding trough, shifting his head toward the manger despite an ensuing stab of pain. He would have wiped his eyes if he could move his hands, but instead he blinked. Through blurred vision he saw baby Jesus lying in the hay, where he had been quickly but safely laid, tightly wrapped, bracketed by the railing, and was now sleeping without a care in the world. Beside the manger, a little row of sheep watched him as if stricken dumb.

Ralph whispered to himself as he faded away: "Holy father and mother of God!"

✳ ✳ ✳

He was wakened a few moments later by the unmistakable wail of a siren. He felt paralyzed and wondered if he was dying. "I can't breathe," he gasped.

Joseph's hands had gently probed his body, unbuttoning his shirt and feeling his side. "Just take one breath at a time, Ralph. In and out. As slowly as you can. You've had a fall. You've broken some ribs. You're

in shock. We're getting you to the hospital. You're going to be okay, Ralph. You're in good hands."

Joseph's words seemed to satisfy the man. His body sagged as his lungs found a shallow rhythm. With a slight but painful turn of his head, he scanned the stable again, from Joseph to Mary to the child in the manger to the livestock and back to Gloria Eagleburger, with her dangling wings and twisted halo. She was spreading over him a blanket fetched from the house.

"Did I ever tell you . . . ," Ralph said, his eyes closing again, ". . . that you look like an angel?" Gloria stared at him in surprise, looking for a hint of sarcasm. But there was nothing in his demeanor but suffering and sincerity.

"*Humph!*" she said. But even her son-in-law the cardiologist noticed that her round face was glowing like a cherub's.

＊ ＊ ＊

As the final shoppers straggled home on December 24, they passed a homemade stable that transported them to another town and another time. There was Joseph waving to them, bidding them a merry Christmas. Beside him, the Virgin Mary did the same. Angel Eagleburger stood nearby, proudly holding baby Jesus. An odd assortment of animals gathered around. And sitting in the rear of the shed was a new addition—a shepherd-come-lately with a cap on his head and a cup in his hand. Ralph Hannaford was there against his doctor's orders, but with the approval of his angel.

His ribs were bandaged beneath his robe and a false beard covered the bruises on his face. He had suffered a terrible fall. But his father's little book had landed beside him with wondrous words of healing and hope. And in the process, Ralph Hannaford had seen the reality of Christmas as truly and as originally as anyone in two thousand years.

He wanted to be nowhere else on this Christmas Eve—just here, sitting on a bale of hay at the back of a makeshift stable, gazing at the baby, sipping his chowder, flirting with his angel, and keeping watch over his flock by night.

Poet Boy

Robert Louis Brendleton lived at the end of a quaint lane just outside Hockley-by-the-Sea, on the outskirts of New Haven. Though neither of his parents was actually British, they listened to the BBC every morning, served hot tea most afternoons at four, and the supper menu on any given night might include Yorkshire pudding, cottage pie, or asparagus mimosa.

Robert Louis's father, Dr. Albert Brendleton, was a professor of Shakespeare and Renaissance Literature at St. Andrews University, where he lectured with a perceptible British accent. Robbie's mother, Dr. Elizabeth Brendleton, taught Victorian poetry at the same institution. Robert Louis was their only child, and he was known for his photographic memory and high grades, though he was a retiring boy and suffered terribly from shyness, timidity, and stage fright. He was happiest when secluded in the reading nook of the library adjacent to his bedroom. There he perused many a quaint and curious volume of forgotten lore.

One Saturday in early October, Robert Louis was in the reading nook, nearly napping, when he heard the Westminster chimes of the doorbell. There were noises of footsteps and door openings and greetings, and Robert Louis heard a familiar voice floating through the house like a piccolo: "Robbie Louie, Robbie Louie, are you here? Come, come. I have exciting news!"

Aunt Clotilda could hardly wait. "Robbie Louie," she said as he entered the room, "I have written a stage play, and I need a well-versed, fourteen-year-old boy as the narrator and chief actor. Do you know such a boy?"

Robert Louis stood speechless, but he shook his head vigorously.

"Well, we have such a boy in this very room, Robbie Louie, for I have chosen you to play the immortal role of the carpenter Joseph, betrothed husband to the virginal Mary."

Robbie tried to reply, but couldn't.

"It's for the Christmas Eve service in the university chapel," she said. "The committee asked me to write an original production, and I have entitled it: *By the Shores of Eternity* by Dr. Clotilda Brendleton. The part of Joseph is written just for you. And you will be pleased to know that Ruby Ascot has already consented to play the role of Mary."

"Oh, oh . . . Aunt Clotilda . . ." —but nothing more came from Robert Louis's mouth.

"I have worked on this stage play for months," continued Aunt

Clotilda. "It has been a long-cherished dream of mine. We will tell the Christmas story, and your opening lines will be: 'By the shores, by the shores of eternity, where time has intersected infinity, a baby was born one night.' Here's the script. I am sure that with your gifts, you'll have it memorized in no time."

"Oh, oh . . . Aunt Clotilda . . ."

And that's how Robert Louis Brendleton found himself standing backstage on December 24, sweating through his costume, peeking at the packed house with its encircling gallery, and wishing he were dead.

But he did *not* die, and at precisely seven o'clock, the curtain rose. Robbie was encircled by a spot of light that seemed brighter than the sun. He was too blinded to see the audience and too frightened to speak. He thought of turning and running, but his feet were glued to the floor. His mind was as blank as if someone had swiped it with an eraser. He tried mightily to remember those opening lines—"By the shores, by the shores of eternity, where time has intersected infinity, a baby was born one night."

But all that came out of his mouth was: "Oh, oh . . ."

After several anxious moments, he heard Aunt Clotilda whispering through the back curtain: "By the shores . . . by the shores . . ."

A single drop of oxygen entered Robbie's lungs. He closed his eyes and blurted out the first words that came to mind:

By the shores of Gitche Gumee,
By the shining Big-Sea-Water,
Stood the wigwam of Nokomis,
Daughter of the Moon, Nokomis.
Dark behind it rose the forest,
Rose the black and gloomy pine-trees,
Rose the firs with cones upon them;
Bright before it beat the water,
Beat the clear and sunny water,
Beat the shining Big-Sea-Water.

He stopped abruptly, and the house was as quiet as the air after an explosion. Then Robert Louis meekly cleared his throat and said, "Henry Wadsworth Longfellow, 1807 to 1882."

There was a muttering of noise from the audience and a sparse bit of applause, followed by additional moments of awkward silence. Then with a mighty shove, Aunt Clotilda sent Ruby Ascot spinning onto the stage.

Ruby was dressed in a pale robe and looked as though she were about to give birth to a large pillow. She seemed frightened, though one

couldn't tell whether it was real or put-on. But in either case, she had no problem remembering the magnificent lines Aunt Clotilda had written for her. "Joseph!" she cried dramatically. "Oh, Joseph, how much farther to Bethlehem? The day is far passed, the night is on the wing, and I am great with child. My mind is perplexed with many an imponderable and unanswerable question, and my heart is sore troubled. What says your heart, oh, Joseph?"

Robbie said nothing, so at length Ruby repeated her last line, and then she repeated it twice more. "What says your heart, oh, Joseph? What says your heart?"

Robbie looked into space and replied:

My heart's in the Highlands,
my heart is not here,
My hearts in the Highlands,
a-chasing the deer;
Chasing the wild deer, and
following the roe,
My heart's in the Highlands,
wherever I go.

Ruby stared at Robbie with bewilderment, but all he said was, "Robert Burns, 1759 to 1796."

It seemed at that moment the entire production might collapse, but from behind the curtain came Aunt Clotilda's strident voice with the next lines: "Listen . . . listen, listen . . ." A flash of recognition came into Robbie's eyes, and he said: "Listen, my children, and you shall hear . . ."

But Ruby cut him off. "Listen, Joseph," she said. "Listen to my questions and reassure my heart. How came we to this point? Whence our divine direction? How came you to lead me down this weary road of Jewish suffering and hope?"

"I shall be telling this with a sigh," replied Robbie after a long pause.

I shall be telling this with a sigh
Somewhere ages and ages hence:
Two roads diverged in a wood, and I—
I took the one less traveled by,
And that has made all the difference.

Robbie was just about to say the words "Robert Frost" when Ruby fumbled for her next line. "And what a difference. All the difference. Yes, and a good difference it is. But, Joseph," she said, recovering, "can we make it onward? I know we can. Look yonder, far ahead of us. Are those the hills of Judea? Are those the mountains of David?"

Robbie looked into the spotlight as if trying to see the mountains of David.

"The mountains they are silent folk," he said at last.

> *They stand afar—alone,*
> *And the clouds that kiss their bows at night*
> *Hear neither sigh nor groan.*
> *Each bears him in his ordered place*
> *As soldiers do, and bold and high*
> *They fold their forests round their feet*
> *And bolster up the sky.*

Just as Robbie was about to credit those words to the American poet Hamlin Garland, Ruby spoke up. "Well, let's go onward," she said with confusion, "onward toward the hills. I can go if you will go, and we can go if I will go, and we shall go if He will help us, and He *will* go . . . and we shall make a go of it."

"Yes," said Joseph with a gulp, "the woods are lovely, dark, and deep, but I have promises to keep, and miles to go before I sleep."

And with that the curtain fell on Act 1.

Since no one could figure out how to keep the curtain from rising for Act 2, the players got into position. The scene was the outskirts of Bethlehem, and this time Mary opened with a long soliloquy, which gave Robbie a bit of time to recover his nerves. He actually listened to her as she recalled the angelic visitor that told her she would bear the Son of God. Ruby ended her speech by nobly saying, "My soul glorifies the Lord and my spirit rejoices in God my Savior, for he has been mindful of the humble state of his servant. From now on all generations will call me blessed" (Luke 1:46–48 NIV).

She looked expectantly at Joseph, whose lines called for tender affirmation. "Oh, Mary," he said, "how do I love thee? Let me count the ways. I love thee to the depth and breadth and height my soul can reach, when feeling out of sight . . . I love thee to the level of every day's most quiet need, by sun and candlelight."

Somehow the words didn't seem quite right, but they didn't seem quite wrong. So the weary couple turned and entered the little cardboard town of Bethlehem.

The play continued through Act 2 with Joseph uttering not a single word that had actually been written for him. Instead the most unexpected snatches of poetry came from his mouth, and somehow they increasingly seemed to fit, if just barely. By the time the Christ child arrived, Robbie had found that his breathing was more normal; it was his memory that was working strangely. It invariably bypassed

Aunt Clotilda's lines, seizing instead on various poems and stanzas and verses long ago tucked away in the photographic files of his internal library.

Some audience members actually wiped away a tear when Robbie quoted the simple lines from the Detroit writer Edgar A. Guest:

Let's be brave when the trials come
And our hearts are sad and
our lips are dumb,
Let's strengthen ourselves
in the times of test
By whispering softly
that God knows best;
Let us still believe, though we
cannot know,
We shall learn sometime
it is better so.

And so it was in the final act that as Joseph stood looking down at the Babe in the manger, there was absolute silence in the church as he recited the ancient words of St. Germanus from the eighth century:

A great and mighty wonder,
A full and holy cure!
The Virgin bears the Infant
With virgin honor pure.
The Word becomes Incarnate,
And yet remains on high,
And Cherubim sing anthems
To shepherds from the sky.
And we with them triumphant
Repeat the hymn again:
"To God on high be glory,
And peace on earth to men."

At last the angels departed, the shepherds returned to their fields, the Babe was carried offstage in the tender arms of the virginal Mary, and Joseph was left in the spotlight for his final lines. No one doubted that Aunt Clotilda had prepared a wonderful closing monologue, but no one heard it that night. Robbie found other words tucked away in the vaults of his memory. They were 1,500 years old, but they seemed as fresh as the youngest child.

Of the Father's love begotten, ere the worlds began to be,
He is Alpha and Omega, He the source, the ending He,
Of the things that are, that have been,
And that future years shall see—evermore and evermore!

O that birth forever blessèd, when the virgin, full of grace,
By the Holy Ghost conceiving, bare the Savior of our race;
And the Babe, the world's Redeemer,
First revealed His sacred face—evermore and evermore!

O ye heights of heaven adore Him; angel hosts, His praises sing;
Powers, dominions, bow before Him, and extol our God and King!
Let no tongue on earth be silent,
Every voice in concert sing, evermore and evermore!

Christ, to Thee with God the Father, and, O Holy Ghost, to Thee,
Hymn and chant with high thanksgiving, and unwearied praises be:
Honor, glory, and dominion,
And eternal victory, evermore and evermore!

❧❀☙

The church was absolutely silent. The audience was enthralled by the story of the Christ child, and no one was ready to break the spell—and so Robert Louis did it for them. For the first time that evening, he smiled; and as he smiled he said:

But I heard him exclaim, ere he drove out of sight,
"Happy Christmas to all, and to all a good-night!"

❄ ❄ ❄

It took a full month for Robert Louis Brendleton to recover his nerves—and a good deal longer for Aunt Clotilda to do the same. But in the town of Hockley-by-the-Sea, the university community of St. Andrews is still talking about the night when the poet boy uttered words from the secret channels of his memory to show us afresh that . . .

. . . by the shores of eternity, where time intersects infinity, a baby was born one night.

Over My Dead Body

A h," said Max Schroeder, his wrinkled face softening and forming a smile, "and have it you shall—over my dead body."

Young Kasper didn't know what to make of his grandfather's well-rehearsed, oft-repeated answer. Nor did anyone else. It was a reply designed to prick the mind while shutting the mouth. And it was spoken indiscriminately to one and all, to the grandson on his lap, to the curator in the museum, to the pope in the Vatican. For everyone on earth, it seemed, wanted to buy, steal, inherit, or otherwise acquire Max Schroeder's most famous work of all—his thumb-in-mouth nativity.

But the old woodcarver would only offer it "over my dead body"—terms that his daughter Johanna didn't like at all. "Why," she once exclaimed, "he's practically inviting a thief to murder him for it."

＊ ＊ ＊

Max had whittled out his career by accident, for as a boy he had needed something to occupy his time while watching his Uncle Karl's sheep in the hills above Lake Lucerne during warm summer months. One day out of boredom—there are no wolves in the Alps—he had extracted his Swiss army knife from the pocket of his knickers and started carving a sheep's face onto the crook of his staff. By age twelve, Max, no fool, was making more money in a week by selling his wooden sheep in Lucerne than he could make in a month by tending his uncle's real ones.

By age fifteen he was supporting himself nicely. By his twenties his artistry was sought throughout central Europe, and by his thirties Max was set for life. One original hand-carved Schroeder Sheep, sold in his own studio in Lucerne, would fetch a very high price indeed.

They were, after all, remarkably winsome sheep. Some were thick with wool, while others seemed lately sheered. Some were old and fat. Others were young and frisky. Most stood on all fours and seemed quite sheepish. But a whimsical few—those in Schroeder's Singular Sheep Collection—stood on hind legs, reading books through wire-rimmed spectacles, playing instruments or cards, spinning hoops, directing traffic, or even giving lectures.

When the French magazine *Le Monde* ran a feature article on "The Shepherd of a Thousand Wooden Sheep," demand for his works doubled, and the price tags on his wooden animals tripled. Every penny went into a numbered Swiss account in Zurich, which Max tended with the diligence of the biblical shepherd who nightly numbered his flock. You might say he was fleecing his public most effectively.

Max was so busy carving sheep and making money that he gave scant thought to romance. But at age forty-two, he met a woman half his age who married him, if truth be told, for his money. She got none of it, for twelve months later she died in childbirth, leaving behind a blond-haired, blue-eyed daughter named Johanna.

Max, however, was effectively distracted from the joy and grief of it all by his work. A popular American magazine devoted its December issue to "The Man Who Traded Wool for Wood." So Max found himself jetting to New York, to Chicago, to Seattle, to Orlando, to London, to Vienna, giving interviews, signing autographs, and making more money. A special showing of Schroeder originals opened in a small but superb museum in Windsor, and Max, amid popping flashbulbs, presented one of his carvings to the Prince of Wales himself. *Newsweek* did a story.

Max's bank account grew, and Schroeder Sheep found their way into the world's most exclusive stores.

Max was in his sixties when Johanna found him slumped over his workbench. It was his heart. His recovery was both slow and depressing, and for the first time in fifty years, Max lost interest in his work.

"But you absolutely must not give up, Father," Johanna said every morning. "Jason and I are going to give you a grandchild, and you mustn't die before he's born. He is due in December."

And Max, looking up from his bed, was surprised at how beautifully comforting Johanna's face was. He had never before taken enough time to study his daughter's face. He had never realized how fair her skin or how blue her eyes. They twinkled and sparkled even when yielding an occasional tear. She proved a good nurse, and within weeks Max was able to sit in his chair. His tools, however, lay forgotten, his carvings untouched, his craving for fame and money diminished.

Kasper was born on his grandfather's sixty-fifth Christmas, arriving thumb in mouth. When Johanna placed the baby in her father's arms, the old man's artist-eye missed nothing. He had never felt such softness or sensed such love. Nor had he ever seen such created perfection. The baby's one hand was balled into a tiny fist to be sucked on. The miniature fingers of the other hand gripped the tip of the granddad's little finger like a vise.

The parish priest arrived at dusk, stomping his feet on the stoop to dislodge the snow. Father Christopher, vicar of St. Joseph's Chapel, was one of those unfortunate people who appear thirty years older than they really are. His face was a spider's web of lines, but each line communicated character. His hair was as white and thin as the cirrus clouds over the Alps. His voice was as clear as a yodeler's call.

Max liked him, and the two struck up a friendship. At Father Christopher's suggestion, the craftsman began reading his New Testament, soon coming to Luke 2.

On the very morning he read the Christmas story—New Year's Day—Max received Father Christopher for coffee. "Why have I never loved this story before?" asked Max. "Why have I never carved Christmas sheep, nor the shepherds watching their flocks by night?"

"Ah," said the priest. "It is because you have so loved the sheep of Switzerland that you have missed the Lamb of God."

"I have been a selfish man," Max confessed. "I have lived for idols of wood. Now I shall live for the Lord Christ. And if the Lord Christ will but strengthen me, I shall create something wonderful for the Great Shepherd whose sheep I have duplicated all my life."

Then taking his checkbook, Max wrote a check. With one slash of his pen, he gave away exactly one-fourth of his fortune. St. Joseph's Chapel was endowed. A new heating system was installed, the old roof was replaced, the organ repaired, the exterior cleaned of a century of blackening soot, and a small elevator installed for the disabled. Furthermore, Bibles were placed in all the hotels of Zurich and Lucerne, an orphanage in Ghana was underwritten, and a Swiss missionary in Costa Rica received a new Land Rover.

Shortly afterward, on January 6, Epiphany, Max woke up feeling that his vigor had returned. "I shall go back to my work today," he announced. For the first time in months, his rugged hands caressed his tools and picked up his neglected wood. By day's end, he had carved a lamb—not a Swiss lamb, but a Judean one. It was larger than most lambs he had ever crafted . . . and more beautiful. Every tuft of wool, each blackened hoof, the rounded ears and glistening nose, the beholding eyes—it was all unequaled. The piece seemed to live. Max almost expected to hear it bleat.

Next came a shepherd with a kindly face etched with lines like a spider's web. Then came Mary, with eyes that seemed to twinkle and sparkle even as a tear ran down her cheek. Then came a sleeping infant, left thumb in mouth, right hand gripping the tip of Mary's little finger like a vise. There followed nine other pieces.

It was a crèche only a heartbeat away from life itself, and all who saw it knew that it was Max Schroeder's masterpiece. When *Newsweek* featured it on the cover of its overseas edition the following Christmas, requests for copies came from all over the world. Collectors, craving it for their displays, offered up to a million Swiss francs. Museums and churches sent curators begging for it.

The answer was always the same. "You shall have it," said Max with a forbearing smile, "over my dead body."

The toughest requests came from family and friends. Johanna hinted. Father Christopher gazed at it wistfully. And young Kasper asked for it outright with childlike simplicity.

"Ah," said Max Schroeder, a friendly glint in his eye, "and you shall have it—over my dead body."

༺❀༻

❊ ❊ ❊

Max's second heart attack took him suddenly in his seventy-ninth year, and all Lucerne turned out for his funeral. In recognition of his tender generosity, he was buried in classic European fashion, under the floor of the church he had endowed, beneath the cobbled stones on which the altar table rested.

Following the funeral, friends gathered for the reading of his will. His money and possessions were allocated as expected, to family and church. There were no surprises, nor had any been expected, for Max had explained his wishes in advance. The only uncertainty lay with the nativity. To whom did Max Schroeder leave the bright-eyed Mary, the thumb-sucking Christ child, the nearly bleating sheep, and the web-faced shepherd?

To Johanna, who had nursed him to health? To Kasper, his only grandchild? To Father Christopher, who had brought him new life? To a great museum where thousands would see it?

In the end, he left it to all of them—by leaving it to none of them.

"And my nativity, I leave to my dear church house, St. Joseph's Chapel, where I lately learned to worship the Great Shepherd, to be displayed every Christmas season until the Christ child Himself shall return."

And so it is that every Christmas, the parishioners of little St. Joseph's Chapel on the edge of Lake Lucerne may see Max Schroeder's crèche with its thumb-sucking Christ child, arranged simply and beautifully on the altar table—over his dead body.

The Telegraph Girl
of Telegraph Hill

t's as though every single soul in San Francisco woke up at the same moment on Christmas Day of 1941. Out of the morning mist, a secret convoy of camouflaged ships sailed through the Golden Gate and into the Bay, and the news spread from house to house like sparks traveling down a fuse. America was fresh into World War II, and the Bay Area was the most vulnerable spot on the continent. Its naval harbor, shipyards, and strategic bases made it a tempting target. German U-boats plied the Pacific, and Californians were nervous about a rumored Japanese invasion.

Normally under these circumstances, the sight of unannounced ships would have caused a panic. Yet somehow on this drizzly Christmas morning in 1941, everyone instinctively understood these were not enemy ships. They were unmarked American naval vessels bearing the wounded of Pearl Harbor to hospitals on the mainland.

That morning all across the precipitous hills of San Francisco, Christmas presents were unopened and breakfasts uneaten as an emotional mass of humanity raced to the wharf—mothers and fathers longing for news of their sons. For more than two weeks, ever since the attack on Pearl Harbor in Hawaii, hundreds of families in the Bay Area had agonized over the fate of their boys. News of the wounded and dead was not forthcoming. The work in the naval yards of San Francisco, home to many brave sailors, went on stoically, but anguish filled many a home and fear gripped many a heart.

The crowds that day were halted at police barricades, but in any event, the ships didn't dock in San Francisco. They took a left turn and disappeared across the bay into the channel leading to Mare Island, the isolated naval base with its well-equipped military hospital. Still, the throngs at Fisherman's Wharf and along the piers were unwilling to go home. They stood silently in the rain and gazed across the gray waters of San Francisco Bay, wondering.

Up on Telegraph Hill in an apartment building at the corner of Union and Montgomery, Rosie Madison was awakened, like everybody else, by the turmoil of the ship sightings. She lived with her mother,

Mary, in a small third-floor flat. It was the stampede of footsteps that awoke her—fellow tenants clattering up the wooden steps outside her window. Throwing a coat over her pajamas, Rosie joined them on the rooftop just in time to see the three ships disappearing around the tip of Angel Island.

"Rosie," said her mom anxiously, "they say those are our wounded Pacific boys, the ones from Pearl Harbor. What if Bud is on one of those ships? What if he's wounded and on one of those ships right now?" Mary Madison, shivering in the drizzle, was wringing her hands so badly that Rosie took them in her own and sought to calm her. But the woman continued breathlessly: "If only we could hear from Bud, it would be the best Christmas in the world, wouldn't it? To know he's all right?"

Rosie, gazing at the foggy bay, said at length, "Well, Mother, I'll just go over and check. I'll go over there to Mare Island and find him."

"Do you think you can get in today?" said Mary with alarm. "It'll be protected like Fort Knox!"

But at age fourteen, Rosie Madison knew she was the one person who *could* get onto Mare Island and who *would* get into its hospital. For her, it would be no problem. "I'll just go over there and see," she said again. "If he's there, by golly, I'll find him. Now come in and have your coffee. I'll be back by sunset."

Releasing her mom's hands, Rosie quickly changed and flew down

the steps, donned her Western Union jacket and cap, and raced from the building two steps at a time. She jumped on her bicycle and coasted down the streets of Telegraph Hill. Taking a right turn on Embarcadero Drive, she glided to a stop in front of the telegraph office at the end of the Harbor House.

"Hi, Mr. Tabatha," said Rosie, sounding as casual as she could. "Any telegrams for Mare Island today?"

"Hi, Rosie, and Merry Christmas to you. Mare Island, huh?" The old telegraph man looked thoughtfully at Rosie. Hesitating a moment, he nodded at the box on the counter. "The overnight boy left those for delivery. There's likely to be some for the Island—Christmas greetings and such."

"Thanks, Mr. Tabatha!" Rosie called, snatching the sealed telegrams and stuffing them into her pouch. She ran out the door, jumped on her bike, circled the building, and glided down the gangplank onto the ferry with thirty seconds to spare. Parking her bike in its place, she went into the passenger cabin and realized she was hungry. She had a dime in her pocket, so she got a piece of cake and a cup of coffee and settled into her seat for the hour's crossing to the naval base at Mare Island. Alcatraz loomed on the port side; then a shaft of sunlight sliced through the clouds and hit the iconic Golden Gate Bridge as it passed on her left. They cleared Angel Island, entered San Pablo Bay, and sped toward the channel.

At first, Rosie had been too preoccupied to notice her fellow passengers. But now she saw them—an unusual collection of people for a Christmas Day crossing—doctors and nurses and medical workers. Rosie realized they'd been summoned to treat the incoming sailors. Everyone spoke in hushed tones, and Rosie's heart rose and fell with the undulating thuds of the ferryboat beating the water.

Her mind drifted to Bud. There was a five-year difference between them; he was nineteen. Their father had died two years ago in a cable car accident, and their mother had never adjusted. She cleaned houses for a living, and Bud had joined the navy to help with family expenses. He'd been stationed in the Bay Area until August, when he was assigned to the USS *West Virginia* at Pearl Harbor. They had heard nothing from Bud since December 7, and Rosie's mother showed signs of a breakdown.

The ferry docked and Rosie was the first off. Approaching the base, she shouted, "Merry Christmas!" to the guards, who waved her through as though she were an admiral. They all knew Rosie—the telegraph girl of Telegraph Hill. She freely came and went every day with personal messages and important wires. Leaving her bike in the rack, she grabbed her pouch and bounced up the hospital steps.

"Hi, Rosie," said the man at the entrance. "Have some wires for us?"

"Sure do," she said, walking past him and into the interior halls. Suddenly her pace slowed. She watched as wounded heroes were being rolled into long dark wards and lined up in hospital beds. Rosie entered Ward AA on the ground floor and took stock of the activity. Some of the new arrivals were moaning, and occasionally Rosie heard one of the boys cry in pain while being lifted from a stretcher into a bed. Soft sobbing came from a few corners. Other areas were silent. A few of the wounded were shouting for attention or calling for a nurse. Rosie hadn't visited a hospital since her father's accident two years before. Now the trauma of those memories instantly merged with the scenes around her. She might have turned back if not for her resolve to learn Buddy's fate.

Rosie noticed a clipboard attached to the end of each bed, and on the clipboard in prominent print was the patient's last name and first initial. She quickly devised a strategy. She strolled systematically through the wards looking only at the names on the clipboards. The combination of her Western Union cap and jacket was like a uniform giving her access to every floor. No one stopped her, so she continued her quest unhindered, from ward to ward, from floor to floor.

She couldn't bring herself to look at the injured boys. Some were badly burned. Some had casts around their limbs. Others were wrapped in gauze. Afterward, Rosie never forgot the smell of their wounds or the sound of their cries.

Up one row and down the next she went—past endless lines of beds, her eyes scanning the clipboards. She searched for hours and had almost given up when she reached Ward Triple-F on the third floor. There she slowed her pace, making sure to scan every name. Barlow, R; Cornhill, D; Rodriquez, J; and then she saw the letters she was looking for, printed on a clipboard at the end of the bed: "Madison, B."

Rosie's hand flew to her mouth. For a moment she couldn't breathe; her feet were frozen to the floor. Then she forced a step, and another. Lying there motionless was a sailor wrapped in gauze, his uncovered face away from her. She gripped the railing of the bed and, summoning her courage, softly said, "Bud? Bud? Is that you?"

A face turned toward her, grimacing in pain.

"Hi, beautiful," he said faintly. "Who are you?"

"I'm . . . I'm Rosie," she said. "Rosie Madison. Excuse me, I thought you might be my brother."

"I wish I were," whispered the sailor. "Who is your brother?"

"His name is Bud Madison. The clipboard on your bed said you are B. Madison, so I thought you might be my brother, Buddy."

Rosie wasn't one to cry, but she felt tears on her cheeks. "He was at Pearl. We don't know where he is now; we don't know if he's alive. My mother is sick with worry. I thought maybe you were him."

"I'm Bobby Madison," said the sailor. Then he added, "Your brother saved my life."

"My brother?" asked Rosie. "Bud? You know Buddy?"

"Sure, honey. I knew Bud real well. We were together on the *West Virginia*. We were always together because of the alphabet. We lined up together. We bunked together. We had chow together. We became great friends."

Bobby paused and shifted his weight with a grimace. "When the *West Virginia* was hit, I was blown off the ship. I landed in the water, and the oil in the water caught fire. It swept over me, and I dove down into the bay as far as I could, but I had to come back up again for air, back into the flames. Your brother saw me fall. He jumped in a lifeboat and pulled me out. He pulled several men out. He saved our lives, and I can still see him, beating back the flames, stretching out his hands into the fire and pulling us out."

"What happened to him? Please tell me."

"I don't know," said Bobby. "The next thing I remember, I was waking

up in the hospital ship at Pearl and everything hurt so badly, and now I'm here. I don't know what happened to Bud. I've wanted to know, but I don't. But, honey, your brother saved my life. I think he saved a lot of lives."

The two were silent a long time. Rosie softly touched the gauze around Bobby's arm. "What was he like as a sailor?" she finally asked. "I often wondered if he liked Hawaii. He said he did. He was stationed there last August, and I've tried to imagine what he was doing."

"Oh, we thought we were in paradise," said Bobby. "We could take a cab to Waikiki for a dollar, and some of us took up surfing. It was beautiful there. Posters were up everywhere—tourist posters all over the island. They had a slogan: 'A World of Happiness in an Ocean of Peace.' That's what it was like. Bud and me, we had a good time. But that's all gone now, ever since that morning."

"And you don't know where Bud is?"

"The last time I saw him was when he pulled me out of hell."

There was a pause, then the sailor asked, "What day is it? I've lost track of time."

"It's Christmas," said Rosie.

"Christmas Day?" Bobby asked.

"Yes, it's Christmas Day, and, well, I have to go. I have to keep looking for Bud, and I don't have much time left. Do you need anything?"

"Yes," Bobby said. "All I have in the world is in that knapsack on the hook. Would you reach in there and find my Bible? If it's Christmas Day, I want to read the Christmas story."

"I don't think you can," said Rosie. "Your hands are all wrapped up."

"If you would read it to me, I'd be much obliged," said Bobby. "I'd like to hear it better than anything in the world."

Rosie's eyes darted to the clock on the wall. She only had thirty-five minutes before the last ferry, but there was no choice. Retrieving the small book, Rosie turned to the gospel of Luke and read from chapter two:

And it came to pass in those days . . . there went out a decree from Caesar Augustus that all the world should be taxed. . . . And all went to be taxed, every one into his own city. And Joseph also went up from Galilee, out of the city of Nazareth, into Judaea, unto the city of David . . . to be taxed with Mary his espoused wife, being great with child. And so it was, that, while they were there, the days were accomplished that she should be delivered. And she brought forth her firstborn son, and wrapped him in swaddling clothes, and laid him in a manger.

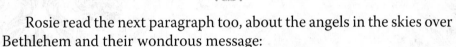

Rosie read the next paragraph too, about the angels in the skies over Bethlehem and their wondrous message:

For unto you is born this day in the city of David a Saviour, which is Christ the Lord. And this shall be a sign unto you; Ye shall find the babe wrapped in swaddling clothes, lying in a manger. And suddenly there was with the angel a multitude of the heavenly host praising God, and saying, "Glory to God in the highest, and on earth peace, good will toward men."

She closed the book and returned it to the knapsack. Finding a handkerchief there, she wiped a tear from Bobby's cheek. Looking at his arms, he said, "Well, now I know what swaddling clothes are."

Rosie smiled. "I have to go," she said.

"I know," said Bobby. "Thanks for reading to me. I think I'll just lay here and pray about it awhile. When you find Buddy, tell him Bobby says 'Hey . . . and thank you.'"

"I'll do that, sir," said Rosie. "You can count on me."

Rosie turned toward the stairwell, glancing as best she could, almost desperately, at every bed she passed. But it was too late. She exited the building, jumped on her bicycle, and raced for the 4:45 ferry, returning home to tell her mother what had happened.

"Well," said Mary, listening to Rosie's adventures, "it's a good sign. At least we know more than we did. Thank God you're a telegraph girl, because your Western Union outfit got us information, and we needed every word of it."

The moment Mary uttered the words "telegraph girl," Rosie jumped to her feet. "Oh!" she cried. "The wires! I forgot about them! I've got telegrams to deliver. They're still in the pouch. I've got to deliver them tonight—all that I can!"

"You can't go out tonight, Rosie. The wartime curfew!"

"Oh, golly!" said Rosie, "Golly! Well, let's sort them for delivery tomorrow morning. That's all we can do."

Rosie poured the handful of telegrams onto the kitchen table, and she and her mother started sorting the envelopes by street location. Picking up one of them, Mary froze. "Rosie!" she gasped. "This has my name on it."

Rosie leaned over and looked. "It's from Washington," she said. "I can tell by the code in the corner." Rosie and her mom looked at each other and back at the wire. When Mary's hand starting shaking, Rosie

POSTAL TELEGRAPH

COMMERCIAL

TELEGRAM

Telegraph-Cable
COUNTER NUMBER.

transmits and delivers this message subject to the terms and conditions printed

TIME FILED.

CHECK.

M.

Send the following message, without repeating, subject to the terms and conditions printed on the back hereof, which

MOTHER. STOP. OK. STOP.
STATIONED DC. STOP. M XMAS. BUDDY

took the envelope, slit it open, and unfolded the page. The words, all in capital letters, were in faded print, as if the Teletype were nearly out of ink. The message was brief: MOTHER. STOP. OK. STOP. STATIONED DC. STOP. M XMAS. BUDDY.

They gazed at the page in unbelief, then their cries brought neighbors running. The joy of Christmas filled the little kitchen as friends and neighbors brought food for a spontaneous celebration. Buddy Madison, feared dead, was alive after all and redeployed to the nation's capital. Finally, after the neighbors left and Mary Madison crawled into bed from sheer emotional exhaustion, Rosie came to tell her good night. "How do you feel, Mother?"

"For the first time in a long time I have hope," said Mary. "What about you?"

"I can't believe I forgot the telegrams," said Rosie. "I could be fired. I grabbed them from the box and didn't give them another thought. And one of them was for us! I've been carrying around the best news in the world—right next to my heart—and I didn't realize it. To think, Buddy got a wire through on Christmas Day, and I almost missed it!"

"Don't worry about it, Rosie. You *had* to be thinking of your brother. With all my heart, I hope those other telegrams are filled with news as good as ours. You can deliver each to its recipient first thing tomorrow. But here tonight, in this home, we have good tidings of great joy."

"Just like on the first Christmas," said Rosie.

"Yes," said Mary. "My son is alive after all, and I know he has saved men from a literal lake of fire. That was his destiny, I reckon. I believe he's coming back as soon as he can. He's going to come back to us, and I believe one day we're going to have peace—true peace—on earth and good will toward men." Mary Madison rested her head on her pillow and said, "I think I'll just lay here and pray about it awhile. I hope you sleep well, honey."

"Me too," said the telegraph girl of Telegraph Hill, "because I've got lots of news to deliver tomorrow."

Five-Quarters of a Mile

he old man had never seen such weather. The Appalachians were blanketed with enough snow to bury the mountain roads, not to mention the cow paths snaking along the hills and the sheds tottering in the fields. Life was at a standstill. Even the snowbirds huddled away in unseen boroughs, unwilling to break the stillness of the forbidding freeze.

Old Zeek arched his feet and stood on his toes, looking through the top pane of his kitchen window. The snow had drifted to eye-level, and he was anxious. He didn't mind being alone in the mountains, but he didn't like being *trapped* here, not one bit, especially with his feeling poorly *and* his being responsible for a six-year-old.

Zeek had enough food in the cupboard and enough firewood on the hillside; that was no problem. But if something happened to him . . . well, he was stranded, that's all there was to it. Stranded with a young child in an old house, the two of them practically buried alive in a snowstorm, the likes of which he'd never seen.

Zeek Miller—short for Ezekiel he guessed, though he'd never been anything but Zeek—lived in an unpainted frame house at the head of a hollow, five-quarters of a mile from the nearest two-lane road. There wasn't a neighbor within hollerin' distance. Until now, that had been just fine. Zeek took a likin' to people well enough, but he liked being alone too. His wife was long gone, swept away in the flu epidemic of 1918. He'd raised Lawrence by himself. Now with Lawrence working up north, Zeek was keeping his grandson, Adam, until better times came.

Adam was a chip off the old block. He loved the mountains like his grandpa did, and Zeek figured he'd one day inherit the old farm. They were buddies, the two of them. They hiked down the mountain every Sunday for church, every Wednesday for groceries, and whenever Zeek had some produce to sell.

Zeek grew vegetables at forty-degree angles on the mountain slopes. He had a small herd of goats he milked for money, but he'd long ago given up the cow, the horse, and all the other critters, except for an old hen that lived under the porch of his little cabin. He was getting tired and didn't want a lot of things to look after.

"Reckon we're stuck here sure enough, Grandpa," said Adam, climbing onto the kitchen counter and peering through the top of the window. "Reckon Pa ain't gonna make it home for Christmas after all."

"No, boy . . . ain't nary a chance."

"Wish he hadn't gone off like that," said Adam for the hundredth time. "What with Ma dead and all; I wish he hadn't gone north. Wish he'd just come back. Wish he'd be here tomorrow for Christmas. But I reckon he ain't gonna come, is he?"

"Well, boy, you know he's a'tryin'," said Zeek. "Wishin's good, but it don't make things happen. This Depression, son, it's wonderful bad. There ain't no work here, no way t'make a living. I told you that a'fore. Your daddy's got hisself a job up there in Ohio, and he's sendin' us money every week. That's why you got shoes on your feet. Now he's gonna be here if he can git hisself here, that's for certain. But this snow, son, this is a true, honest-to-goodness blizzard, that's what it is. Now you fetch me a match, boy. It's gettin' dark, and I reckon we best light the lamp."

Adam scrambled off the counter and ran to the matchbox on the wall. "I'm gettin' cold again, Grandpa," he said, returning match in hand.

"Yeah, me too, Adam," said the old man, striking the match and lighting the wick of the old lantern. The clock on the wall struck five times, and Zeek, glancing at it, thought of supper. "After I fetch us some more firewood, son, I'll stir us up some grub. Just look at that wood box. It's 'bout near empty again, and I just filled it at lunchtime. Reckon I'd best try to fill it up before it's plumb dark outside."

"I'll help you, Grandpa."

"No, boy, you best stay in. It's too cold for a child to be out a'doors. You'd nigh freeze t'death. You listen for me and, when I holler, you open the door real wide and let me back in. I'll have m'hands full."

Zeek's old boots, cracked with age, sat by the door, and it took him a while to stuff his feet into them and lace the strings. He shoved his arms into his tattered wool coat, then pulled his cap over his thick, gray hair. When he opened the door, a freezing gust rattled the house and made him shudder. Ducking outside, Zeek banged the door behind him and trudged through the dusk toward the woodpile.

He knew why the firewood was burning so quickly, and it bothered him. The wood was too dry. He'd been stopping at the upper end of the woodpile and carting last year's wood back to the house, and it was so dry it burned like paper. The box by the stove emptied as fast as he filled it. But the old wood was lighter, and Zeek was having trouble carrying the heavier wood.

That worried him. He'd always worked like a horse and, even at seventy-six, he was hale and hearty, or so he thought. He'd been gathering firewood for seven decades, and he knew fire logs like a scholar knows history.

But something was wrong, and Zeek felt winter in his bones. Two days ago he'd had a spell while shoveling snow from the path that led past the woodpile and on to the outhouse. That pathway was crucial. "We don't have to go to town," he'd explained to Adam. "We don't even have to go to the church house; but we do have to git to the firewood and down to the outhouse. Those are the 'portant things—the firewood and the outhouse. Gotta keep a path open, or we'll be in real trouble."

But his path clearing had exacted a heavy price, and Zeek had been sick to his stomach and sore in his chest ever since. His arms felt weak, and he winced with a catch in his lungs. His breath was labored, and as he trudged to the woodpile, he tried to veer down toward the newer wood. But his feet slipped beneath him, and he found himself standing at the upper end where he selected an armful of dryer, lighter wood. Four sticks and that just about did it. He couldn't lift another piece.

Approaching the house, Zeek took a deep breath and called as loudly as he could, "Adam! Open the door." The pain struck his chest like a bullet, hitting him point-blank, slicing through his flesh, into his lungs, through his heart. His legs gave way. Firewood tumbled onto his head, and he tried to break his fall with one hand, clutching his chest with the other. The dusk turned to darkness, and a paralyzing cold fell on him like an avalanche...

Somewhere in his unconsciousness, Zeek felt he was drowning in a frozen lake, high in the mountains, swimming upward toward the ice that covered the surface. Finally he broke through the water and through the ice, and he opened his eyes. Adam peered down at him anxiously with red eyes and a face as white as the snow that surrounded them.

"What happened?" Zeek asked, wincing as pain shot through him like circuits of fire.

"You fell something awful, Grandpa," said Adam. "I like to a'never pulled you through the door."

"How long ago?" said Zeek, struggling with every word. He tried to lift himself onto his elbow, but couldn't. "How long have I been like this?"

"A might spell," said Adam. "I've just been a'sittin' here beside you. But, Grandpa, the firewood's nearly gone, and it's gettin' mighty cold."

Zeek lifted his head. It was dark now, the only light being the flickering flame of the oil lamp casting deep shadows that quivered on the walls. Suddenly the gears on the old clock moved and the striker hit the coils. One . . . two . . . three . . . and on to ten. Ten o'clock, and cold.

"That firewood you brought, I got it outta the snow. I've been puttin' it in the stove, but it's gone now," said Adam, "and the fire's 'bout out. I reckon I'd best go and get us some more wood."

"No," said Zeek, wheezing, speaking with labored breaths. "No, Adam, you can't; it's too dark . . . too bad . . . cold. Might not make it back. If you git lost, you'd freeze yourself to death."

"But, Grandpa, there's a path. You dug it for us."

"Ya can't go out there," said Zeek. "The woodpile, it's too far. It's icy. You might fall, might not make it back . . . git lost . . . too dark . . . it's cold . . ."

"But, Grandpa, we're gonna freeze in here. We gotta keep the fire a'goin'."

Zeek's head dropped back onto the floor. The pain was running down his arms, but the boy was right. If the fire went out, they'd freeze before morning. But if the boy went out, he'd freeze before midnight. Zeek closed his eyes and prayed for help.

"Adam," he said at last, "Adam, burn the kings."

"What, Grandpa?"

"Those three kings over there. Go get 'em. Throw 'em in the stove, one at a time. Go on, you gotta do it now before the fire goes out."

Adam glanced to the large nativity in the corner of the room, shrouded in the shadows. Each piece was made of hickory and was about a foot tall, about the size of a piece of firewood. Zeek's grandfather had whittled the pieces out many years ago, one per winter, until the entire set had been finished. The wood was well seasoned and heavy, and was the closest thing Zeek had to an heirloom. For many years, he'd made a little display in the corner of the flowerbed during Christmas. But this year the snow had come early, so he'd hauled the figures from the barn and set them in the corner of his little room.

"Grandpa, you love those ol' kings. We can't burn 'em."

Zeek, grimacing with pain, lifted himself up on an elbow to look the boy in the eyes. "Now you listen to me real good. You take and haul those kings to the stove and throw them on the fire, one at a time. You've got to do it, Adam, right now, before the fire goes plumb out."

Without another word, Adam obeyed. Zeek sunk back onto the floor and drifted into unconsciousness. The next time he opened his eyes, the clock was striking twelve times. Midnight. Adam was curled next to him asleep, an old blanket spread over the two. Using one hand, Zeek shook the boy. "Adam, wake up. Adam! You've got to tend the fire again."

"What's that, Grandpa?"

"Adam, throw the sheep on the fire. Do it now, Adam. It's getting colder."

Adam rubbed his eyes, rolled over onto his feet, padded to the corner, and like a heartless shepherd threw the innocent lambs into the stove, arranging them with the poker. He watched a few minutes as the wood slowly caught fire, casting off a heat that baked him in delicious warmth.

At two o'clock, the three shepherds went into the furnace, one at a time—like Shadrach, Meshach, and Abednego, but without a Fourth Man to deliver them.

When the clock struck four, Zeek again shook his grandson awake, this time to throw Joseph onto the fire. Fortunately, Joseph was a portly fellow of unusually hard hickory, and it took him a while to give up the ghost. But by six o'clock, it was Mary's turn to be consigned to the flames.

By seven o'clock, the sun was coming up, but it was a bitter morning and the fire was nearly out. Into the stove went the manger. Now only the Christ child remained, like a lone figure lying on the floor in the corner of the room, the sole survivor of the night's holocaust. Adam fetched some bread and milk, and Zeek nibbled it before giving the final order.

"Adam," he said, "throw baby Jesus in the stove."

"But, Grandpa . . ."

"Just do it, Adam."

Adam loved the baby Jesus, and this Christmas he had plucked him off his manager every day to hold him and play with him. Jesus was smaller than the other figures and easier to manage. His figure was so personal and lifelike, and the expression on his face was so strong and happy. Adam opened the door and, as carefully as he could, trying not to burn himself, he gently placed Jesus on the hot coals. The poker remained propped against the wall, for Adam knew he couldn't jab at this piece. The baby's eyes peered back at him from the glowing enclosure of the old stove, lying not in a manger of hay, but on a bed of embers.

"Sorry 'bout this," Adam whispered, closing and latching the door. It was done. The flames started to lick the wood like a serpent, and soon Jesus was ablaze in the flames of the old stove. Adam felt a tear slide down his cheek as he turned away. He ran to his grandpa, still lying on the floor, buried his face in the old man's chest, and cried, not only for Jesus, but for his grandpa whose face had never seemed so old or wrinkled or gray.

"It's gonna be alright," said old Zeek, lifting his hand to stroke the boy's hair. "Baby Jesus is gonna save us, you just see. Just think of the heat and the light he's giving right now." Zeek closed his eyes, and his hand rested silently on the boy's hair.

❄ ❄ ❄

Zeek's next conscious thought was hearing the gear of the clock wind up to strike again. This time he was unable to count the strokes,

and when he tried to open his eyes, his vision was blurred. But he felt linens around him, a mattress under his bones, and a pillow beneath his head. A large hand seemed to be squeezing his own, and a deep, familiar voice fell on his ears.

"'Bout time you stirred, Pop. Git those eyes of your'n open. I'm heatin' ya some goat's milk. You know how that settles your stomach. It's Christmas Day. Adam, fetch me that glass of milk for Pop."

Zeek felt a hand lift his head and a glass touch his lips. He took a sip as best he could. The voice continued, "I've been here a while, but I walked back down to the highway and sent for the doctor. He'll be comin' directly, I reckon. You're gonna be alright. I've got the fire goin' real big; it's nice and warm in here, and you'll be fine."

Zeek opened his eyes a little wider and tried to speak. A soft smile flickered then faded on his weathered face, and he closed his eyes to rest a spell.

After Christmas that winter I returned with my dad to Ohio, leaving my grandpa under the deep midwinter's snow of his Tennessee mountains. His old place lay dormant and abandoned for many years, but not forgotten. Now I've returned, for my life has come full circle. Many winters have passed since that cold Christmas long ago, but I often relive the never-to-be-forgotten night, five-quarters of a mile into the hills, when the Christmas story went up in flames and the Christ child perished in the fire to save my life.

A Blue Danube Christmas

he river Danube meanders two thousand miles from the Black Forest in Germany to the Black Sea in Romania, linking ten European nations and four capital cities. One of those is Bratislava, the political and economic center of old Slovakia. Although the Communists are gone, their legacy hangs over the city like smog. You can hear it in the creaking trollies and taste it in the grit that hangs in the air. But there are signs of life. The Old Town, dotted with quirky statues and whimsical sculptures, has become a stopover for travelers. Boats plying the Danube from Vienna to Budapest now dock in Bratislava so tourists can try Slovakian goulash and purchase local art.

As observant guests notice, Bratislava is also home to a large dog population—purebreds and fleabags, leashed and wild. This is a story of one of them, Blue, a mutt whose ancestry included a Euro-mix of Irish Setter, German Shepherd, and Swiss Mountain Dog. Blue belonged,

more or less, to Anton, a thirteen-year-old with floppy hair and an easy grin; and Anton belonged, more or less, to Ilya, his older brother who ran a storefront café on Strakova Street.

One day in December Ilya and Anton went looking for a Christmas tree—a free one—for the café. They scavenged the Danube Valley a kilometer or two from their small flat. Blue ran on ahead with doggish energy, pausing periodically to dig for bones. The brothers found a reasonable facsimile of a tree lying in the mud along the banks of the Danube. It had toppled off a barge. They swished it in the river, gave it a good shaking, and lugged it to the tiny café, propping it in the corner. It yielded no holiday cheer.

"Anton," said Ilya with a discouraged shrug, "we need a woman's touch. This tree, it needs some help. Take Blue and look for tinsel. Some lights, huh? Who knows? People discard things. Look for dropped packages and abandoned parcels. Check the trash cans and keep an eye out for workers putting up decorations. You never know what people leave behind, huh?"

So the boy and his dog traipsed through the alleys and avenues

until they came to the medieval streets of the city center. They watched workmen stringing festive lights across the central square and down its evocative lanes. Shopkeepers were doing the same with stores. The effect was magical. The heart of Bratislava glowed. An accordion player bellowed out carols while hawkers sold roasted chestnuts from smoking barrels on cobblestoned corners.

As Anton and Blue sauntered past souvenir stores, art galleries, and touristy restaurants, the boy searched for a strand of discarded lights and Blue sniffed the air for discarded bones. A stream of drool trailed behind him.

Suddenly Anton saw a woman cross the sidewalk before them. Her voice sounded like the jingle of sleigh bells. "Petrov," she said liltingly, "if you have a moment I'd like to show you the sculpture I'm taking to the cathedral tomorrow. The unveiling is at noon, at St. Martin's, and I'm just getting it finished. I've labored on it for months."

The woman bounded the single step of the shop and pressed through its gingerbread-style door, followed by an older man in a craftsman's apron. The woman reminded Anton of a mannequin. He guessed her to be his brother's age, about twenty-six. She was clad in skinny jeans, black leather boots, and a gray woolen trench coat encircled by a dark fabric belt. A red scarf looped around her neck, and two glittering earrings matched the sparkle in her eyes. Her perfume fragranced the air like a bouquet of lilies.

Anton couldn't keep his eyes off her as she disappeared through

the door. Painted on the window were the words: "Alžbeta's Fine Art: Religious Themes."

"Blue," whispered Anton, "did you see her? Come here, boy. Sit."

The boy and his dog parked themselves on the stoop leading into the store, and Anton leaned against the resisting door, pressing his back against the wood and glass until the door inched open ever so slightly. Putting his finger to his lips, he said, "Be still, Blue."

From inside the shop, the conversation continued. "Here it is, Petrov," said the woman. "Just two pieces. The manger is carved from a small block of fine Carrara marble. And here is the Jesus figure. He's utterly unique, carved from bone."

"It's exquisite, Alžbeta," replied the aproned man. "It looks like ivory; it has the same soft color and smooth texture. I've read about bone carvings and seen a few, but I've never attempted one. Where did you get the bone?"

"It's the thigh bone from a camel that died of natural causes at the Hungarian Zoo," said the woman. "I bought it from a dealer from Budapest. The marrow had already been extracted, and the bone was soaked and seasoned, which makes it easier to carve and craft."

"The Christ child in fine bone carving!" Petrov exclaimed. "And from a camel bone! Perhaps—who knows—it was a camel descending from the dromedaries used by the Magi themselves!"

"I doubt that, Petrov," said the women with a laugh, "but bone carving does go back to prehistoric times. The craft is as old as civilization, and it's the closest we can come to ivory, now that elephants are endangered. Notice how the ivory-like color of the bone accentuates the rose tones in the marble."

"So delicate," gushed the man. "The display at St. Martin's will be magnificent."

Listening through the crack in the door, Anton heard almost every word. He was curious about the perfumed woman in the black jeans whose voice rolled through the air like sleigh bells. But the afternoon was deepening, and it was cold. An occasional wisp of snow brushed his cheek. Cramming his hands into his pockets, Anton pressed himself against the door, knees to chest, feet squeezed together, elbows stuffed beneath his undershirt and coat, head cocked with ear to door.

Anton didn't realize another person was inside the shop at that moment, an obese tourist who was loitering as his wife browsed nearby. The man suddenly saw he'd lost track of time. A glance at his watch propelled him toward the exit, and with a cursory nod to Alžbeta, he yanked the door.

Caught off guard, Anton rolled backward into the shop like a circus clown, his imprisoned hands useless. He tumbled back in a half somersault at the feet of the exiting man. A set of paws hurtled over him. The dog's tail swept past his face. In a blur of confusion, the boy twisted around just in time to see Blue flying across the shop like a cannonball and leaping onto the counter.

Alžbeta screamed. Petrov yelled. Snatching the Christ child, Blue juggled the bone in his mouth, clamped his teeth into it like a vise, and growled. He vaulted from the counter, feet pawing in midair. He landed off balance, straightened himself, and barreled toward the door, cutting between the legs of the heavyset man like a train throttling through a tunnel. The tourist lost his balance and crashed to the floor. The ground shook. Statuary trembled on their shelves. Only evasive action saved Anton from being crushed. But in his peripheral vision, he saw his dog bolting into the street like brown lightning.

"Jesus!" cried Alžbeta. "That dog has my Jesus! Somebody stop him!"

A pair of black leather boots leaped over Anton as Alžbeta ran toward the open doorway. From the stoop, she pointed down the street, shouting, "That dog has Jesus, my Jesus! Somebody catch that dog!"

Shoppers looked up at the commotion, tourists stopped their conversations, and a handful of local citizens took out after Blue. Anton jumped to his feet and joined the chase, with Alžbeta close behind. Blue was sprinting on all fours, ears back, tail straight, bone clenched

in teeth. He headed instinctively toward the river, where he felt safest. The pursuing mob gained size and speed like a snowball.

Meanwhile, back at the shop, Petrov had the presence of mind to call the police. A large contingent of them was finishing security detail at a political rally on the right bank of the river. They headed toward the bridge leading to Old Town.

Back on the left bank, Blue tore down Strakova Street, galloped by Ilya's café, and rounded the massive corner of St. Martin's Cathedral.

"He's heading to the bridge!" someone shouted. Sure enough, Blue had his eyes focused on the great UFO Bridge crossing the Danube. This bridge is the most iconic structure in Bratislava. It's called the UFO Bridge because Soviet engineers, wanting to create a dramatic piece of structural propaganda, designed a melodramatic suspension bridge topped by a sky-high restaurant in the shape of a flying saucer.

Arriving at the bridge, Blue avoided the traffic lanes and dashed up the steps to the pedestrian walkway. At the landing, he stopped and laid his treasure on the concrete. He was panting heavily. The pursuing throng slowed as they turned the corner of St. Martin's. Catching sight of the dog, they bolted toward him like stampeding horses. Snatching up his bone, Blue bounded up the remaining steps and tore across the bridge. He was halfway across when he saw a flood of blue uniforms rushing toward him. The officers, too, were waving their arms and shouting.

Blue stopped in his tracks, trapped. His teeth held the bone tightly while the corners of his eyes surveyed the impasse. His pursuers were converging toward him from both directions. He felt the vibration of the bridge as it trembled with moving traffic and running feet. The hordes were forty meters away on both sides, and advancing fast. Thirty meters. Twenty. Both mobs stopped ten meters on either side of Blue, and the shouting died down. The dog emitted a threatening growl. His hair bristled. His ears were back and his muscles taut. No one moved.

Anton, in the vanguard of the pursuers, took a step forward, speaking softly, his hand outreached. On the other side, a police officer took a corresponding step. Blue dropped the bone and the officer burst toward the spot. To Anton, the next moments seemed frozen in time. Grabbing the fallen bone, Blue turned toward the railing, crouched like a cat, and leapt up with one smooth motion. His feet touched the top of the railing, which he used for leverage to fling himself into thin air. His paws drilled the air like an Olympian, nose aimed toward the water. He descended with the symmetry of a Strauss waltz, plunging toward the swiftly flowing Blue Danube.

Anton gripped the railing and screamed as Blue hit the river far below and disappeared beneath its inhospitable currents. The crowd, standing in slack-jawed horror, emitted a collective gasp.

"I've never seen anything like that," said a man nearby.

"Like a suicide jumper," said another.

"Doggone," said a third man.

For the longest time everyone gazed into the river, eyes searching for any sign of dog or bone, but Blue never resurfaced. Finally, the mob began to disperse. At last, only Anton remained at the railing, shivering in the cold and in the biting wind, yet unwilling to leave. He turned and leaned against the railing. Slowly his back slid down the wall until he sat on the bare concrete, his face buried in his hands and knees. He could not control the tears.

At length he caught a whiff of lilies. Peeking through his fingers, he saw a skinny pair of jeans. The woman in the trench coat towered over him, arms crossed, face impossible to read. "Was that your dog?" she asked.

"Yes," said Anton.

"Well, that was my Jesus," she said.

"Yes, I know," sniffled Anton. "I'm sorry about that."

"I loved my Jesus," said the woman.

"I loved my dog," said Anton.

"Yes, I can tell," said Alžbeta as she studied the trail of tears cutting through the dirt on the boy's face. "I'm truly sorry for your loss. Come on now. I'll take you home."

"I can go home by myself," said Anton.

"Yes, but I'm going to take you anyway. You need something warm in your stomach. You're freezing."

"My brother's a cook," said Anton.

"Good," said Alžbeta, "because I'm hungry and cold too. Now let's go."

Within the hour, Alžbeta was sitting at a stark table in the small café with its bare Christmas tree. Her nerves seemed to have lost the worst of their edge. She was warming herself with a steaming bowl of homemade chicken soup from Ilya's stove.

Anton, on the other hand, found no comfort in food. He played listlessly with his spoon and occasionally salted his broth with a tear. But even in his lethargy, he couldn't help noticing there seemed to be a little spark flittering through the air like a lost lightning bug. Ilya was trying hard to be casual; Alžbeta was trying equally hard to be angry.

She ordered another bowl of soup and asked how old the coffee was.

"I'll make a fresh cup for you, huh?" said Ilya.

"Thanks," said Alžbeta without expression. "I just don't know what to do now. I'm supposed to debut an original crèche tomorrow at St. Martin's, and the Christ child is missing. He's gone for good, like that dog of yours. I have many other pieces—mostly in marble—but nothing appropriate to the set."

"Well, at least your dog's not dead," said Anton dejectedly. He didn't mean it unkindly, but he hadn't experienced this kind of grief since he was a small child.

"Hey, Anton," said Ilya, "come on, cheer up. There's always hope, huh? Dogs have a way of showing up again. They're like cats. They have eight or nine lives, eight maybe."

Anton looked at Alžbeta and asked, "You saw him jump. Do you think he'll come back?"

The young woman gazed at the boy and shook her head. "Truthfully, no. But I do think I know how you feel. I lost a pet I loved very much. I was your age. It made me feel as empty as . . ."

Her voice trailed off as she rose and turned toward the door.

"As empty as a manger with no Jesus, huh?" said Ilya, finishing her sentence. "Here, let me get the door for you. Thanks for bringing the boy home. We're sorry about what happened."

But Alžbeta didn't move. She simply looked at Ilya curiously, her thoughts elsewhere, on the words he had spoken. "An empty Christmas," she said. "Of course that's what it means. An empty Christmas."

Anton and Ilya looked at each other and shrugged. But the woman spoke again. "You've caused me a terrible problem," she said, "but you could help make it right. In the attic of my shop I've got boxes with marbles and carvings and sculptures that I've made through the years. Will you help me search them tonight? I need some pieces, and likely as not they'll be in crates in the back. I have till noon tomorrow to assemble an empty Christmas."

"Well, yeah, we'll help of course, huh? It's the least we can do, seeing what's happened. We'll go with you," said Ilya. He grabbed his coat, nudged Anton from his chair, turned off the stove, and reversed the sign on the café door from "Open" to "Closed." Braving the flurrying snow, the three lean figures, like silhouettes, wound their way through the now-darkened streets of old Bratislava.

That night, rummaging around in the attic, they *did* find a solution.

For the next month, visitors filed past an odd nativity scene in an alcove of St. Martin's Cathedral. The display was ringed by a heart-shaped strand of holly, exquisitely carved from green Italian marble. Inside the sculpted holly were several disparate items: a miniature version of a monarch's throne, a small marble manger, a wooden cross, and an open tomb. No explanation was given except for a small caption that read: "The Empty Christmas."

The Empty Christmas

Most people eyed the display intriguingly and passed by, wondering what had happened to the baby in the manger. But there were other displays, other crèches, and the crowds who threaded through the dim aisles and alcoves of St. Martin's tended to forget each display as they came to the next.

The days passed. Midnight Mass and Christmas Day were soon over, and all over Bratislava the decorations came down.

Alžbeta, Ilya, and Anton packed up the display on New Year's Day and hauled the items back to the Old Town shop. Most of the objects were returned to the attic, although a few were retained to display in the store. After everything was tidy, Ilya invited the little team to his café for the best goulash in Slovakia.

"I do think it was successful, don't you," asked Alžbeta, "even though it attracted little notice and most people didn't get it? I feel it was the most authentic Christmas display in the room."

"Yeah, I liked it," said Ilya. "Why do you think most people didn't get it, huh?"

"Most people don't truly understand Christmas," said Alžbeta, sopping up the last traces of goulash with her remaining slice of boiled bread. "They never think beyond the Babe in the manger. But I was taught, and I yet believe, that Christmas is about an empty throne, an empty manger, an empty cross, and an empty tomb—all of which fill our empty hearts."

"Yeah," said Ilya. "It's a circuit. I was able to explain that to a buddy at midnight mass."

"Yes," said Alžbeta. "It was a round-trip ticket with stops along the way. The Christ child left the throne for the manger, the manger for the cross, the cross for the tomb, and the tomb for the throne. He left blessings behind at every stop. He emptied Himself so we might be filled. That's the true story of Christmas."

Ilya nodded in agreement. "It makes perfect sense, huh? You understand that, don't you, Anton, huh?"

Wiping his mouth, the boy cocked his head and flashed a smile. "Yeah, I get it. I thought it was the best display in the church," he said. "I thought it was cool. How 'bout you, boy, what do you think?"

Curled in the corner where the ragged tree had recently stood, Blue thumped his tail and gnawed on a bone.

Nativity Seen Smiling

amon never wanted a big December wedding, but Claire, spurred on by her mother, had insisted. And Claire had never wanted to go to Puerto Rico for their honeymoon, but Damon's travel agent friend had given them the four-day trip as a wedding present—and Damon, never one to pass up a bargain, had insisted.

And so, wilted and weary beyond words, the nervous couple had dashed from the wedding to the airport for the red-eye from Denver to Miami, then raced to the connecting flight from Miami to San Juan, and finally were driven by an overpriced taxi to Old San Juan itself.

They arrived irritably at midmorning to find their room at the Hotel Presidente still occupied by the previous guest. While waiting in the lobby, Claire drank a large glass of pulpy orange juice—which contained sixteen ounces of something lasting thirty-six to forty-eight hours. She was instantly good for nothing but the bathroom.

A frustrated Damon had spent the afternoon napping at the pool. His fair, unlotioned skin had broiled in the Puerto Rican sun, and the resulting blisters had left him so sore he could barely be touched.

The unhappy couple had snapped at each other endlessly, taken their meals in silence, and thwarted all efforts at honeymoon bliss. Even their tour of the Puerto Rican rain forest had been a washout. Now they were down to their last day.

"It was a terrible mistake," Damon muttered, standing in his boxers by the window during a sudden downpour.

"The trip?" asked Claire.

"Yes," said Damon. "The trip. The wedding. The whole thing. I'm not saying I don't love you, but we couldn't have started things worse. I'm still exhausted from that wedding your mother staged. The grand ballroom, three photographers, five hundred guests, two hundred poinsettias, and a Colorado Supreme Court justice. I'm still a bundle of nerves about that. Nothing was missing except the partridge in the pear tree."

※

"It would have been a beautiful wedding," Claire retorted, red hair disheveled, "if you hadn't glowered through the whole thing. And it would have been a wonderful honeymoon if we had gone to Aspen or Vail like I wanted."

With a curse, Damon threw his suitcase on the bed, opened it, and began throwing in his clothes. "Let's go home," he said. "At least, I'm going. You can do whatever you want."

But, of course, it was still a long time until their evening flight. When the rain paused mid-afternoon, it seemed advisable to escape their close quarters. Barely civil, they left the hotel and wandered through the bazaars and markets, inspecting baskets, bowls, carpets, and carvings, looking for just the right item to take home as a souvenir. "Like, maybe, a machete from the rain forest," muttered Damon. But as everything triggered an argument, they were ready to give up when they heard an eager . . .

"Buenos días, señor and *señora."*

They turned to see a small, dark-skinned man wearing an apron and flashing a bone-white smile.

"Enter into the shop of Felipe Chavez, *por favor*. Look at my carvings. They are very beautiful. I make you good price."

It was his countenance that drew them through the beads and into his shop. But Felipe's smile dimmed as he glanced at their faces. "Ah, *señor* and *señora*," he said, "I do not know many things, but one thing, I know the faces. I can read the lines in the brow, and the mouths and the cheeks and the chins. I can read eyes. And I see an unhappy story, no? Felipe Chavez, he does not like unhappy stories. He likes the ones that are happy ever after, no?"

Damon and Claire glanced at each other, shifted their weight, and shrugged. "We haven't felt well," mumbled Damon.

"No," said Claire. "Damon got sunburned, and I've been a little . . . uh, sick."

"Oh," said Felipe, "you perhaps had the orange juice at Hotel Presidente? Ah, well," he said, smile returning. "No problem. It is past. Now, *por favor*, look at my carvings. They are works of art. You will find nowhere on the island their equals. They should be in the National Museum, but, alas, I am undiscovered. I make you good price. *Comprende?"*

Claire and Damon began exploring the little shop. It was drab and dusty. As they moved from one shelf to another, Felipe followed them like a beggar, switching little spotlights on and off as needed, explaining the distinctive features of each piece.

The figures were all carved from lightly colored wood, and most were about ten inches tall. The bodies were rough hewn, but the faces were exquisite—all of them smiling. There were bullfighters and firefighters, Incas and Indians. All smiling. Even the Spanish conquistadors were smiling. There were stallions and eagles, soccer stars and saints. And all were smiling.

"Your characters," said Claire, "they have such happy faces."

"Ah, *bien*, you have noticed," said Felipe. "I told you. I read faces; that is my hobby. As I work by the window, I watch people passing by. They come, they go, they do not know that Felipe watches them. And when I see a smile, I quickly chisel it onto one of my figures. All these smiles in my shop, they once belonged to people."

As Damon and Claire continued browsing the little, unswept shop, they both saw it at once, a nativity set, displayed by itself at the end of a shelf.

"Oh," said Claire, "I've never seen a crèche like this. Everyone is smiling. Look, the angels seem so happy, and the shepherds. Even Joseph and Mary have smiles. And, oh, look! The Christ child, he is smiling too."

"Of course," Felipe replied. "Why not? It is *Feliz Navidad*—Happy Christmas. Tidings of joy to the world. Lord Jesus, He, only, gives joy *grandé*."

Then Felipe added quietly, "Lord Jesus, he would bring joy *grandé* to you."

"We'll take him," said Damon.

"You'll take Lord Jesus?" asked Felipe.

"Yes," said Claire, "the whole set—Mary, Joseph, the shepherds, and maybe a few extra sheep."

"*Sí, señora.* I will wrap them. It is eighty dollars."

As Damon pulled out a hundred dollar bill, another customer entered the shop. Felipe became distracted, making change and boxing the crèche while scurrying around, turning tiny spotlights on and off, and hoping for another sale.

As Claire and Damon strolled to the hotel, they almost felt like newlyweds after all. But the euphoria was short-lived, for the ensuing rush to the airport and dash to their plane soured their spirits again. The flight was crowded and hot, and they returned home in foul moods.

Things grew even worse when they opened their souvenir only to discover that in his haste, Felipe had failed to put the Christ child into the box. The holy parents were there, the angel, the shepherd, and his flock. But Jesus was missing.

Claire began crying as she arranged the pieces on the mantel. Without the Christ child, the crèche seemed hollow and hostile. Even the smiles on the figures lost their charm.

"It's a parable," Damon said grimly. "Our marriage is a mess, God doesn't care, and I don't know what to do about it."

For a week neither spoke much, nor was there much tenderness or intimacy between them. Damon seemed lost in thought. Claire chatted every day with her mother and went about Christmas shopping. But she, too, pondered their future.

On Christmas morning a fresh layer of snow covered the Rockies. The sun was bright, and the air was clear. Claire woke first, and when Damon stirred an hour later, he found her sitting by the tree with the animated eyes of a child, fingering her presents. Christmas music was softly playing. Gathering a blanket around him, Damon joined her cross-legged on the floor.

"Open mine first," Claire eagerly said.

"No, you open mine first."

"No, mine."

"Well, all right," said Damon. "I will. It's so small and thin, I can't imagine what it is." Tearing away the paper, he opened a small, flat box, discovering inside an envelope. It contained a card that looked very much like a wedding invitation. It read: "This is to invite the bearer to a small, private wedding to be held in the snow by the old pine tree on the north side of Stone Church, December 25th, three o'clock."

"I don't understand," said Damon.

Claire looked at him, eyes glistening. "I guess you could say it's a proposal," she said. "I want to start our marriage over again. I called Pastor Humphry about it. He's agreed to let us renew our vows this afternoon. No parents. No photographers. No fancy clothes—just you and me and Pastor."

Claire thought she had anticipated Damon's every possible response, but she wasn't prepared when he started chuckling and shaking his head. "What's so funny?" she asked. "What is so funny about that?"

"It's not really funny," said Damon. "It's just that . . . I, uh . . . well . . . here! You open my gift."

Damon held out his gift—equally small and flat—and watched her open it. Inside was a postcard of a little village nestled at the foot of the Rockies.

"I thought we could use a few days in Aspen," said Damon. "Our reservations start tomorrow. I guess . . . well, we can pack for our honeymoon right after our wedding. Isn't that the way it's supposed to work?"

Claire was speechless.

"I felt we needed a new start too," Damon explained. "It's never too soon for a second honeymoon—and never too late. We've got to believe that."

"I do believe it," said Claire, tears coming. "Especially at Christmas. Do you remember what Felipe Chavez said? 'Lord Jesus, He, only, gives joy *grandé*.'"

"Speaking of Felipe Chavez," said Damon, a new tone in his voice, "I'd almost forgotten. It came in yesterday's mail."

Reaching behind the tree, he drew out a small package wrapped in brown paper and bearing special delivery stamps. A wonderment filled Claire's face. She ran for scissors, cut the string, and slit open the box. Inside was a note:

> *I found this after you left. So sorry. The clerk at the Hotel Presidente is my cousin, and he gave me your address so I hope it arrives by Christmas.*
>
> *Felipe Chavez*

Damon and Claire drew from the box the baby Jesus and carefully restored him to his rightful place on the mantel.

"It's a parable," said Claire.

Damon nodded. *"Feliz Navidad, señora!"* he said, wrapping his arms and his blanket around her. "Or should I say, *Felipe Navidad!*"

And if only Felipe Chavez could have seen them then, he would have carved happy faces all day long.

Gabriel's Cry

<hr>

The Virgin Mary sat on the edge of a stone wall near the ancient well of Nazareth. Looking into Gabriel's face, she studied his expression. "I have news for you, Gabriel, angel of God," she told him. "Good tidings of great joy! A baby is on the way, and you're going to be a father!" Hearing those words, Gabriel's dark eyes widened and, throwing up his hands, he opened his mouth and gave a great cry.

✳ ✳ ✳

It had started on a drizzly evening the previous year, when Emma Snider had inserted her key into the back door of East Side Tabernacle in New York City. The church sat across from Tompkins Square in Alphabet City, which is the only part of Manhattan with lettered streets instead of numbered ones. This section of town is neither poor nor prosperous, neither safe nor dangerous, neither black nor white nor brown. It is a vintage melting pot, and Emma liked it here. She played the piano at the Tabernacle each Sunday, and although it was only August, she was already preparing for the scheduled Christmas concert.

Hitting a switch on the wall, Emma delivered a single pool of light around the instrument. Her fingers bore down on the keys, sending determined chords echoing off the walls and evaporating into the dark timbers of the old wooden ceiling. She reveled in the majestic notes of Handel's *Messiah*, with the words bouncing in her head: "For unto us a Child is born; unto us a Son is given."

As the last strains faded into the rafters, Emma was startled to hear a single set of hands clapping. Whirling around, she saw the silhouette of someone sitting cross-legged halfway down the aisle.

"Don't be afraid," said the voice, seeing her alarm. "I'm harmless; I was just listening. Your music is so beautiful I would pay to hear it."

"Who are you?" Emma asked tensely.

"I'm Andy," said the young man. "Don't worry. I was just listening. I love the piano."

"Andy who?" asked Emma.

"Andy Melendez."

"What are you doing here, Andy Melendez?"

"Well, I sleep here."

“No,” said Emma sharply, apprehensively.

“Not always; just sometimes. The pews are padded.”

“You don’t have a key.”

“Well, I don’t need a key.”

“Are you homeless?”

“No,” said Andy. “I have a mother who lives in Brooklyn. I stay with her whenever I want.” He paused, then continued, “You know, Mr. George Frideric Handel would be downright pleased to hear his notes coming from your piano.”

“How did you get in here?” asked Emma.

“It’s not easy to reduce Handel like that. Is it your own arrangement?”

“Yes.”

“Reductions are tricky. You managed to compress the whole spirit of Handel’s orchestration into eighty-eight keys and ten fingers. It was marvelous.”

“I’ve been working on it,” said Emma. “What are you doing here? How did you get in?”

Andy, still cross-legged in the aisle, shrugged. “I learned things growing up,” he said. “I can get in; I can get out. And, ah, I guess I

should be going. But take it from me, a little more practice and I'll be listening to you one day at Lincoln Center." His voice was shy and soft and friendly, and before Emma could say anything else, Andy was on his feet and out the front door.

Emma thought long and hard about reporting Andy, but she was somehow touched by his affable manner. His knowledge of music intrigued her, and his compliments didn't hurt either.

Perhaps she should have been uneasy when she returned to the church two nights later for her regular practice, but somehow she wasn't. Truth be told, she was a little disappointed when there was no sound of clapping hands as she finished her piece.

Nor was Andy there the next week. Or the next. Emma had given up on seeing him again, and truly she didn't know whether to be relieved or disappointed. But one night a month later, as she sat at the piano, she sensed she wasn't alone. "Andy?" she called.

"Hi," came a gentle voice from the darkened room. "Mind if I listen? Don't be alarmed. I'm harmless. I've never hurt a soul. I just want to sit here on the floor and let your music lift my spirits."

"Do your spirits need lifting?" asked Emma.

"Yes, they do."

Emma started playing, and she played as though at Lincoln Center. When she finished, he applauded and thanked her. This time he didn't leave, but Emma did. Feeling a flicker of fear, she quickly rose from the bench and slipped through the rear door, turning off the light behind her. Still, she couldn't keep a slender smile off her face.

Over the next two months, Andy was more likely to be in the church than not. Before and after practice, they chatted across the room, Andy sitting cross-legged in the dark aisle and Emma on the stage in the spotlight. Andy never stepped onto the stage, and Emma never stepped off it.

And that is how they dated.

Emma learned that Andy's mother was a woman of questionable reputation in Brooklyn. Andy had never known the sailor who fathered him; he had grown up knowing how to hide and to stay out of the way, and he was good at it. She learned he often slept in Tompkins Square or Central Park. He knew how to camouflage himself like an Army Ranger. He knew how to evade the police by sleeping among the tree branches in a thin, nylon hammock. Occasionally he even spider-webbed himself to the tops of trees like a mountain climber sleeping against the cliffs.

One evening Emma asked what he did for a living. "Well, I'm a carpenter," he replied. "I remodel apartments on the Upper East Side. I

think I'm pretty good at it." They talked about his work, and Andy perked up as he described projects he was working on and the craftsmanship he put into his work.

Then Emma wanted to know what Andy did for fun, how he spent his weekends. "I hang around the East Side," he said, "sometimes in the Village or in Brooklyn, listening to jazz bands. Whenever I can, I take in a concert at Lincoln Center. I like that stuff too."

Before she could stop herself Emma asked a question she instantly regretted. "Why don't we hang out Saturday?" she said. "It'd be fun to spend the day together, visiting the parks, listening to music."

It was as though she had taken a step too far. Andy looked down, fidgeted, shrugged, and seemed at a loss. Finally he spoke so softly that Emma had to strain to hear him. "Well, Emma," he said, "you know, I really don't have much to offer you. It's fun talking to you, and I love listening when you practice, but we're different people. I'm pretty ragged. That's what my mom always told me. My mom calls me Raggedy Andy. I drift about, sleeping wherever I want. I don't have a roof over my head. Sometimes I'm hungry; sometimes I'm thirsty. I've been beaten up on the streets. I've been teased and taunted all my life. I don't really worry about it, but people don't understand me, and I don't blame them. I'm even a mystery to me. I don't know what I believe, or who. I don't know where I live, or why. You're too good for that."

Unfolding his legs and gripping the edge of a pew, he rose to his feet and lumbered toward the door.

"Andy," said Emma, "wait a minute! Don't go. I don't think you're ragged at all. I like being with you. I enjoy talking to you very much. You're an unusual person; you're a conundrum."

"A what?"

"A puzzle," she said. "But you're a gentle puzzle. You must believe in yourself; I can tell you do. You must believe in something."

"Well, no," he said, reaching the door, "I don't. I feel hopeless, but it's in a happy sort of way."

"Andy, you have lots of hope inside you. My goodness, you're in church more than I am. You sleep here sometimes. You could sleep anywhere. You could camp out in some of those apartments you're remodeling. But you like sleeping under God's stars and sleeping in God's house. Doesn't that tell you something?"

Andy, his hand on the door, said nothing.

Emma continued. "I know from my practice sessions that churches

are mysterious places at night. I feel a strange Presence in this empty room at night when I'm practicing the piano. I'm not talking about your presence, though I've learned to sense that too; I know when you're here. But I'm talking about God's presence. I feel it every time I play Handel and think of those words, 'For unto us a Child is born; unto us a Son is given.'"

Andy half shrugged, glanced a final time at Emma, and pushed against the door.

"Will you at least come to the concert?" shouted Emma. "After my part of the program, the pastor is going to talk about Christmas." But the door was already closing behind the shy, elusive young man. He was gone, and there were no more Andy sightings after that.

Emma had never experienced such a long and lonely December. New York was unusually cold that year, and she found it hard entering the sparsely heated church night after night to practice. But she persevered, and finally the evening came for the Christmas service. Shifting nervously at the piano, Emma looked across the audience, hoping to see Andy. But the glare of the floodlights obscured the faces.

All she knew was that no one was sitting cross-legged in the aisle. When she finished her recital, the applause thundered through the room, and then Emma's elderly pastor rose to finish the night with a homily about the birth of Christ. He tapped the microphone, cleared his throat, and said:

The Babe of Bethlehem, whose birth we celebrate, is the conundrum of history—a puzzle, a problem, a prince whose crib was a manger and whose genealogy was stained by men and women of questionable reputation. As a child He was teased by those questioning the legitimacy of His birth. As a youth He was taunted by brothers who doubted His mission. As a man He bore the scorn of those seeking His destruction. Yet the power of His presence astonished the masses, and they said of Him, "What manner of man is this?"

He was a working man, a ragged carpenter with neither a roof above His head nor a pillow beneath it, sleeping under the stars or in borrowed beds; His robe a blanket, His nightlight the moon.

For thirty-six months He drifted about doing good and telling stories. He never hurt a soul. He healed the sick, taught the masses, fed the hungry, walked across the seas, and preached the good news. Wherever He went, the miraculous broke out—at weddings, at funerals, on the land and on the lake, on the mountainside and in the city streets. He became the help of the helpless and the hope of the hopeless. He turned water into wine, and with bread and fish He fed a multitude; yet He Himself was sometimes hungry, and in His death He cried out in thirst.

He is mystery in every way: Obscure in birth, humble in youth, hardworking in life, flawless in character, gentle in spirit. Yet hated, rejected, beaten, and crucified—though His condemner said, "I find no fault in Him" and His executioner said, "Surely this was the Son of God."

He was buried in a donated mausoleum. Yet His tomb, guarded by Roman soldiers, was opened by heavenly agents—and found empty. And for two thousand years we can say that all the angels of heaven, all the demons of hell, all the stars in the sky, and all the men of the earth have never understood the influence of this gentle child in swaddling clothes who was laid in a manger with no crib for a bed—Jesus Christ our Lord.

The church was silent as flickering candles cast haunting shadows against the walls. The old man's words sank into the hearts of the worshipers. Then the silence was broken by the sound of a single set of hands clapping.

❄ ❄ ❄

Things moved quickly after that. Andy and Emma were married in February, and by early December they were heavily involved in the next Christmas pageant at the Tabernacle, which this year was to be a Christmas play. Emma was chosen to play Mary. Andy, of course, was happier out of sight behind the scenes. He built the sets—the stone wall by the well of Nazareth, the little town of Bethlehem, and the manger in a cave. He was particularly proud of his manger, for it was secure enough to actually serve as a cradle.

The only problem occurred at the dress rehearsal, when the man playing the part of Gabriel had clients show up unexpectedly at his brokerage firm. At the last moment Andy was compelled to dress up like Gabriel as a stand-in at the rehearsal. And that's when Emma decided to break the news. To everyone's amusement, she turned the tables on the dark-haired angel. "I have news for you, Gabriel, angel of God," she told him. "Good tidings of great joy! A baby is on the way, and you're going to be a father!" Hearing those words, Gabriel's dark eyes widened and, throwing up his hands, he opened his mouth and gave a great cry.

❄ ❄ ❄

The little boy arrived right on time the following August. He was born exactly on the second anniversary of that strange night when Emma had sat in a pool of light and played "For unto us a Child is born," unaware of her silent listener. The baby was plump and healthy, and there was no question about his name. He was called Gabriel Andrew Melendez.

Andy rummaged through the basement of their apartment building and hauled out the manger he had so carefully crafted the previous December. Bringing the child home, they placed him within its narrow confines, wrapped in a snuggling blanket.

"Gabriel in the manger," Emma said as they peered down at their son. "Now that's a twist in the story."

Andy laughed. "Yeah," he said, "I like that. Gabriel in the manger. It's sort of like . . . well, the Christmas story all mixed up." He leaned over the crib and jostled his son's belly. "What do you think of that, Gabe?" he said. "You're a conundrum, just like your dad."

And at that, Gabriel's little eyes widened and, throwing up his hands, he opened his mouth and gave a great cry.

Christmas Joy

A true story as told by Joy Christofferson about a cherished memory
from her childhood during the Great Depression.

J oy Christofferson grew up in tiny L'Anse, Michigan, on Keweenaw Bay of Lake Superior, where the average December temperature is 17 degrees. She spent her childhood enduring the Depression of the 1930s, when Christmases were hard. Her father, Arthur Salness, had moved to L'Anse from Minnesota, having grown up there in a family of nine children. Leaving school after the fifth grade, Arthur went out to earn a living. He left home shortly thereafter—pushed out—to work on the railroads and in the iron mines. He met and married a schoolteacher named Dora, and the family moved to L'Anse in Michigan's Upper Peninsula, where Arthur worked in Henry Ford's lumber mills. Ford owned a half million acres of nearby forestland to provide wood for his cars, since every Model T contained about 250 square feet of lumber for the floors, frames, hubs, and body.

Money was always scarce for the Salness clan. Jobs were fleeting, and in the Depression years Arthur was often without work. He traveled to other towns, found jobs wherever he could, and sent the money home. Dora and the four children raised potatoes, corn, cabbages, lettuce, peas, beans, tomatoes, and other produce, which they canned and stored for winter. A potbellied stove and kitchen range heated the house, fueled by firewood gathered from scraps in Mr. Ford's woods.

Dora's sister, Lois, lived in Chicago. She was an unmarried schoolteacher with a steady but small income, and she sometimes sent the family boxes of discarded clothes, which Dora transformed into new pants, skirts, and dresses. Aunt Lois was eccentric, adventurous, and generous. Sometimes she sent a dollar or two extra. But in those days teachers often experienced unpaid stretches till funds were available to make up their salaries, so her ability to help was unpredictable.

Joy's family entertained themselves throughout the winters by poring over the Sears and Roebuck and Montgomery Ward catalogs. Father thumbed through the tool section; Mother studied the cloth and patterns; the sisters looked at the dresses; and the brothers ogled the bicycles and air rifles. As for Joy, she looked at the doll beds. She had a doll but it slept in a box, and Joy thought it should have a real bed. She also drooled over the dollhouses and thought, *Wouldn't it be fun to play house with that beautiful two-story mansion with an indoor bathroom?*

One December day, Father came home with exciting news: "I stopped at the post office, and we have a package. It's too big to carry, so I'll have to take the car to get it tomorrow." The family owned an Overland ("I think it was a 1916 model," Joy says. "Dad had to crank it to start it, and in the winter he drained the radiator every night so it wouldn't freeze. We only took it out for special trips.")

Well, everyone was terribly excited about that box, and very curious. They guessed it was from Aunt Lois, since nothing had been ordered and no packages were expected. They wondered if it was full of old clothes or new presents.

After work the next day, Father lugged the mysterious crate into the house and everyone gathered around. It was from Sears and Roebuck. Aunt Lois must have ordered them gifts.

Mother opened the large box and took out the first item—a box of chocolates filled with luscious interiors. This was new to the children. All they'd ever had was cheap candy from the Five-and-Dime. "Each of you may pick one piece," said Mother. "We want this to last."

The next item was a large bag of nuts—not just peanuts, but walnuts, pecans, almonds, and Brazil nuts. "Poor Aunt Lois," they exclaimed. "She shouldn't have spent her hard-earned money on us like this."

"What's next?" cried the children.

To their amazement, it was a full set of electric lights for the Christmas tree. Father always cut down a tree and brought it inside for

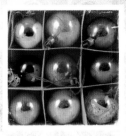

the holidays, but they'd never had lights. The Salness tree was decorated with chains of construction paper, homemade paper snowflakes, and handmade drawings. The strands of electric lights left the whole family momentarily speechless, but there followed beautiful ornaments and bulbs and balls—the likes of which the children had never seen. The rest of the box contained an assortment of gifts, including four pairs of mittens just right for the four youngsters.

When Joy awoke on Christmas morning, she ran to the beautiful tree with its electric lights, bulbs, and balls. Underneath she found a cradle for her doll, handmade from a grape basket and lined with soft pink flannel salvaged from an old pair of pajamas. She also found a dollhouse under the tree, a homemade two-room, two-story version assembled from scraps of wood and finished with leftover paint. On that Christmas, Joy lived up to her name as the whole family celebrated the goodness of the season.

The next day they wrote an effusive letter of thanksgiving to Aunt Lois and the letter was mailed. Imagine their surprise when Aunt Lois replied by return post, saying she knew nothing about the gifts. "I didn't send that box," she wrote. "We didn't get paid before Christmas, and I couldn't send anything this year."

Who, then, had sent the presents?

After puzzling about it a while, Mother said to the children, "I'll write to Sears and Roebuck and ask them to send me the name of our benefactor. We must thank that generous person. I had better use ink for this one. Get me the inkwell and pen and a rag to wipe it on."

They composed the letter and posted it, and a few days later the response came:

Dear Mrs. Salness:

The box that you inquired about was sent to you by error. It was ordered by Arthur Salinen, not Arthur Salness. Please pack up all the items and send them back, or send a money order for the cost of the merchandise.

That created quite a dilemma, and the family hardly knew what to do. With the Depression at its worst, the retailer might as well have asked for a thousand dollars. The family treasury was empty. "But Father and Mother agreed on this reply," says Joy:

Dear Sears and Roebuck:

We ate the candy and nuts, and the decorations and other items have been used and can't be resold. We don't have any money to pay for these things. If you didn't send it, and no one else did, it must have been from God and we cannot turn down His gifts.

⁂

The mighty Chicago retailer apparently agreed, for the matter was dropped and only the memories and mittens were left. For Joy, those memories have lingered a lifetime, and to this day she still calls this her best Christmas memory ever—the year God sent an impoverished family a box of undreamt-of gifts, and Mr. Sears and Mr. Roebuck were simply the delivery boys.

Sugarplum and the Christmas Cradle

ost of the twists and turns of life can never be anticipated, and few things work out as planned. Even a simple task like building a cradle can be as unpredictable as driving on a rainy night without wipers. This is one such story—a tale of a cradle lovingly made but never used, and of a baby lovingly conceived but star-crossed in birth.

The initial news created something of a stir. Some couples wait a while before having children, but not J.B. and Sugarplum. They'd no sooner put their wedding gifts away in the cupboard than they started working on the nursery. News of their love child set tongues a'wagging, and the in-laws were none too pleased.

"You're too immature to have kids," said J.B.'s mother. "Why not wait a couple of years? I'm too young to be a grandma."

J.B. just smirked and said nothing.

Sugarplum did the same when Uncle Adam said bluntly, "This is too soon. You've not been together long enough." The mother-to-be simply patted her stomach and quipped, with a mischievous smile, "It's too late now!"

Down at the work site where the construction of a new building was underway, J.B. took a lot of ribbing from his buddies. "You sure didn't waste any time," said one. "How long you been hitched?"

"Why wait?" said J.B. with a crescent-moon smile.

"When's the kid due?"

"In January or February; we'll find out soon. We can hardly wait for him to get here."

"Oh," cackled the men, "so it's already a *him*!"

The young couple, in their joy, took no offense, harbored no anger, and absorbed all the kidding with enviable grace. Soon family and friends were immersed in planning showers, choosing names, making blankets, and stockpiling diapers.

J.B. was certifiably the world's most excited father-to-be, but that wasn't the bad part. The sickening thing was how he treated Sugarplum—not how *badly* he treated her, but how *good* he was to her—like a lethal tonic of molasses.

Sugarplum, don't you think you'd better rest a while?

Sugarplum, you lie down while I do the dishes.

Sugarplum, you just prop up those twinkle toes and let me rub your feet.

Sugarplum was currently his favorite moniker for his brown-eyed wife. During their courtship he'd called her Babes, but that didn't seem to fit. So he went through a series of other babyish names, like Baby Cakes, Baby Doll, Babe-o-mine, and Babylicious, but none had stuck. So he went on to the C's: Cuddles, Cupcake, Cupid, and Cutie. Later it was Precious, Princess, Pumpkin, and Puffins.

Finally he'd gotten to the S's, and that's when he'd found Sugarplum, and now she was Sugarplum morning, noon, and night. Truth be told, it was getting a little sickening, even to Sugarplum, who felt she was being sugar-pummeled to death.

Sugarplum, let me sweep the floor. I'll go to the market. Let me lift that pot. I'll make the bed. Let me do it.

She put up with it for weeks—it had been so much worse since the start of her pregnancy—but the final straw broke when she doubled over with nausea and vomiting, and J.B. hovered over her like a first-year medical student.

Sugarplum, I can't stand to see you like this, with this awful morning sickness. I think that if you have to throw up, I'll just throw up too.

And he actually did!

That's when she put her foot down. "J.B.," she declared, "I love you, but you are driving me crazy. You've got to find something to do around here besides following me around morning and night. You need an outlet for your energy."

"But, Sugarplum . . ."

"That's enough *Sugarplumming* for now. Find something useful to do while I finish supper—and make sure it's out of my sight! Why not clean out the workshop? I'll call you when the lamb chops are done."

And that's how J.B. started working on that ominous cradle. He meandered to the garage, shifted around some boxes, found an oak plank, and the idea came to him in a flash of inspiration. Yes, it should be oak and not pine, because this wasn't a job for a soft wood. This cradle would be molded from beautiful hardwood with rich grain patterns and unique designs. His creativity went into high gear, and before supper the entire project had come together in his mind. Even for a woodworker like J.B., a cradle is a challenge to build. It's one thing to have the skills and tools to do the job; it's another thing to know how to design furniture and have the knowledge of construction techniques required for the task.

Of course, J.B. could have ordered a set of plans, but he wanted this cradle to be one-of-a-kind, because it was for his one-of-a-kind child. For the next several days, Sugarplum found herself blissfully neglected as J.B. spent every spare moment before and after work at the kitchen table, sketching, erasing, drawing, and designing the project. It was to be a very traditional cradle—not one that hangs on a frame and swings like a pendulum, but an open trough that sits low on the floor, with rockers on either end and a wooden covering rising at one end as a canopy for the baby's head. No spindles to trap the baby's arms or legs, but a closed-in, tiny sanctuary for the little soul.

It had to be deep enough for a small mattress, of course, and big enough for the baby to use for some time. Every edge had to be rounded and smooth, with no rough spots, cracked boards, or splinters. And no nails or screws. Everything would be dovetailed and hand-pegged.

Most important, it had to rock smoothly and gently, but not too much. "Can't have it tipping over when the kid's old enough to stand up in it," said J.B., erasing a line and reducing an angle. After determining the radius for the rockers, he began finalizing his sketches, and soon Sugarplum saw much less of him, to her enormous relief. Before work, after work, and on weekends, he was sawing, chiseling, routing, assembling, and sanding. Along the way he salvaged the scrap pieces of leftover wood, carefully shaping and sanding them into a beautiful set of building blocks. But most of his attention was on the cradle.

"I've got to get it done in plenty of time," he told his buddies down at the construction site. "I've found a nontoxic finish, but the stain has to dry for about a month so there's no danger of the little fellow getting any fumes. Of course, he might come early, so I need to have the whole thing finished by late November."

By now, Sugarplum was starting to miss her man, and she was relieved when he reentered her life full force. After all, she was great with child, as they say, and for the first time, she really did need his help.

"I feel like you've been away on a trip," she told him.

"Well, just you wait till you see it. It's been a labor of love," he said. "It's for you as much as for our kid. You know what they say: 'The hand that rocks the cradle rules the world.' Besides, with all the children we're gonna have, that cradle will have a long career. Then the grandkids will use it, and the great-grandchildren. I feel like I've created an heirloom, a masterpiece."

"Well, are you going to keep on talking about it," asked Sugarplum, "or are you going to let me see it?"

Fetching a dishtowel from the kitchen, J.B. covered Sugarplum's eyes and led her into the nursery. When he removed the rag, there it was—a cradle so beautifully designed, so stunning in its simplicity, that Sugarplum wept the moment she saw it. The grain patterns of the wood were enhanced by the rich oaken colors of the dark stain, and the rockers were so smooth and perfectly aligned that it practically rocked itself. A little galaxy of six-pointed stars was painted onto the end of the cradle, but otherwise it was unadorned. A golden blanket was folded over the mattress, compliments of J.B.'s mother who was a gifted seamstress.

Sugarplum sat on a stool beside the little bed and caressed it, running her hand across the rich lumber. In her mind's eye, she could see her little one sleeping peacefully within its secure walls. J.B. knelt beside her, and it seemed natural for them to ask God to bless the tiny baby whose birthday was only weeks away. The palm of J.B.'s rough hand gently rested against Sugarplum's stomach and, right on cue, he felt the baby move as though already part of the family—which, of course, he was.

It was the calm before the storm. As it happened, for all the work that went into it, the cradle was never used and their little fellow never laid his head within its enclosure. The nursery remained empty, the tiny house was vacated, and the young couple's lives were traumatized.

The culprit was a registered letter that arrived at bedtime, addressed to one Joseph ben Jacob, ordering him to Bethlehem as part of a national census. Against all advice, Sugarplum went with him, mounted on the family donkey.

Visit
RobertJMorgan.com/12Stories

About the Book **About the Author** Get a FREE Christmas Story Send a FREE E-Card

12 Stories of Christmas
Sharing the Smiles, Heart, and Hope of Christmas

Robert J. Morgan
Foreword by Dr. David Jeremiah

Rediscover the Wonder of Christmas!

For the past twelve years, pastor, bestselling author, and master storyteller Robert J. Morgan has written original heartwarming stories for the members of his church on Christmas Eve. Now these twelve stories are yours in one beautiful volume, to be cherished year after year as a family tradition or for personal inspiration.

Read More *Buy it Here!*

Watch the FREE Christmas Story "That's My Boy"

Sign up for Rob's E-Newsletter, and recieve a free link to view *That's My Boy* as read by Robert J. Morgan.

Name   Email Address   *Sign Up Here!*

Robert J. Morgan

Robert is Pastor of The Donelson Fellowship, a best-selling author, and a Gold-Medallion winner. With over 25 books in print and over 3.5 million in circulation, his products in electronic and audio format number hundreds of thousands. He is also a staff writer for Dr. David Jeremiah and Turning Points Magazine, and has many articles published in other leading Christian periodicals. His books have been translated into Spanish, Dutch, Russian, Chinese, Indonesian, Korean, French, and Polish. He is also a regular contributor to The Huffington Post.

Read More

Send a custom E-Christmas Card!

Merry Christmas

Complete the short form to the right to send your friends or family a free E-Christmas Card!

Customize your E-Card's message

Sign your E-Card

Recipient's email address

Every card includes a link to one of the *12 Stories of Christmas!*

Send My Card!

RJM

Share The
12 Stories
of Christmas

Visit www.robertjmorgan.com for access to exclusive free *12 Stories of Christmas* extras, such as:

- *Video of Robert Morgan reading the story of "That's My Boy!"*
- *Free e-cards to share with friends and relatives*
- *Beautiful Christmas desktop wallpaper*
- *and more!*

ROBERT J. MORGAN
B O O K S

THOMAS NELSON
Since 1798